GRAMMAR
CONNECTIONS
3

Lynda Berish

Sandra Thibaudeau

Maria De Rosa Wilson

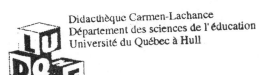
Prentice Hall Regents Canada, Scarborough, Ontario

CANADIAN CATALOGUING IN PUBLICATION DATA

Berish, Lynda, 1952–
    Grammar connections

ISBN 0-13-333304-3 (v.3)

1. English language—Textbooks for second language learners.*
2. English language—Grammar.
I. Thibaudeau, Sandra, 1943–   . II. Wilson, Maria De Rosa.
III. Title.

PE1128.B485 1995   428.2'4   C94-931523-0

Prentice-Hall, Inc., Englewood Cliffs, New Jersey
Prentice-Hall International, Inc., London
Prentice-Hall of Australia, Pty., Ltd., Sydney
Prentice-Hall of India Pvt., Ltd., New Delhi
Prentice-Hall of Japan, Inc., Tokyo
Prentice-Hall of Southeast Asia (Pte.) Ltd., Singapore
Editora Prentice-Hall do Brasil Ltda., Rio de Janeiro
Prentice-Hall Hispanoamericana, S.A., Mexico

ISBN 0-13-333304-3

Executive editor: Clifford J. Newman
Managing editor: Marta Tomins
Production editor: Elynor Kagan
Production coordinator: Sharon Houston
Design and layout: Joseph Chin
Illustrations: William Kimber
Cover design: Olena Serbyn

Printed and bound in Canada

5   99 98

To the many students we have had the pleasure of teaching over the years, for the inspiration their many questions have provided.

Contents

Vocabulary	Ten-Minute Grammar Games
Transportation	Do You Remember? Participle Chain
Household articles	Find Someone Is It True?
Sports, sports equipment	Sentence Ends An Activity Survey
Games, activities, hobbies	Stump the Expert Small Talk
Emergencies	Hopes and Wishes Three Wishes
Office equipment and supplies	The Agony Column Regrets
Clothing	Solve the Problems

Topics	Ten-Minute Grammar Games
Music, art, and entertainment	Medieval Puzzles A Soap Opera
Medicine and the body	Objects and Places How Do You Do It?
Food	Tell Me the Future Find Someone
Jobs and professions	Quick Draw Sentence Ends
The city	Puzzles

To the Teacher

Grammar Connections 3 provides a quick review of intermediate structures and systematic coverage of more advanced grammatical structures. It is geared towards students who have a strong functional base in English but need to complement their language development with attention to accuracy.

The units of the book provide clear explanations and examples of the structures. Each unit follows a sequence of activities that take students through several steps.

To begin, a warm-up "What Do You Know?" exercise activates students' knowledge of, and interest in, the grammatical structure. This activity is followed by "Understanding Grammar," a section of explanations and comprehensive practice exercises that offer stimulating variety as well as opportunities for pair work and group interaction.

Through this central section of each chapter, a picture dictionary runs across the bottom of each page. Its purpose is to support general language development and expose students to specific fields of vocabulary that are of interest at the upper intermediate and advanced levels. Students need to match listed words to the pictures. A section called "Vocabulary Challenge" reviews these words at the end of the unit.

A section of "Ten-Minute Grammar Games" provides a variety of simple games and puzzles as a lively way to practise structures that have been taught. Teachers and students will appreciate activities that involve everyone in a few minutes of fun at the end of a grammar lesson.

Each unit concludes with a "Test Yourself" section that allows students to test and monitor their own progress. Every fifth unit follows the format of TOEFL® grammar tests to provide a review of the structures and vocabulary of the preceding four units. Answer sheets for these test items are provided on pages 193–197. Complete answer keys for all the exercises are included at the back of the book.

Simple Past Tense vs. Present Perfect Aspect

What Do You Know?

Take the 50-Verb Challenge!

Complete the chart with the base form, the simple past (affirmative) form, or the past participle.

Present	Past	Past participle
1. awake	awoke	_____
2. arise	_____	arisen
3. be	_____	been
4. beat	beat	_____
5. become	_____	become
6. _____	began	begun
7. bite	bit	_____
8. _____	blew	blown
9. break	_____	broken
10. bring	brought	_____
11. choose	_____	chosen
12. come	came	_____
13. _____	did	done
14. draw	_____	drawn
15. drink	drank	_____
16. _____	drove	driven
17. eat	_____	eaten
18. fall	fell	_____

19. _____   flew   flown
20. forbid   _____   forbidden
21. forget   forgot   _____
22. forgive   _____   forgiven
23. _____   froze   frozen
24. get   _____   got (gotten)
25. give   gave   _____
26. go   _____   gone
27. grow   _____   grown
28. hide   _____   hidden
29. _____   knew   known
30. ride   rode   _____
31. _____   rang   rung
32. rise   rose   _____
33. run   _____   run
34. see   _____   seen
35. shake   shook   _____
36. show   _____   shown
37. shrink   _____   shrunk
38. sing   sang   _____
39. _____   spoke   spoken
40. spring   _____   sprung
41. steal   stole   _____
42. stink   stank   _____
43. swear   _____   sworn
44. swim   swam   _____
45. take   took   _____
46. tear   _____   torn
47. _____   threw   thrown
48. _____   woke   woken
49. wear   wore   _____
50. _____   wrote   written

a glove compartment a gearshift windshield wipers a steering wheel tires		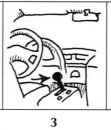			
	1	2	3	4	5

Understanding Grammar

UNDERSTAND: **Simple Past Tense**

Use the simple past tense to describe actions that were completed in past time. Use the simple past tense if you can answer the question "when," either because:

a) a time marker such as **last weekend**, **yesterday**, or **three years ago** is used.

   We met some terrific people on our trip **last summer**.

b) both speaker and listener share knowledge of when the action took place.

   Did you and Jill enjoy your trip? Yes, we had a great time.
   (Both people know which trip, and when it was.)

Simple past tense verbs can have regular or irregular forms, but only in the affirmative form.

The regular form of past tense verbs is formed by adding **d** or **ed** to the base form of the verb. Sometimes spelling changes are required. See Appendix 1, page 189 for spelling rules.

The irregular forms of past tense verbs must be learned by heart.

TEACHER'S BOX: Many verbs that describe everyday activities have irregular forms. However, most other verbs are regular in the past tense.

a turnstile
a fare box
an escalator
tracks
a platform edge

6   7   8   9   10

4

A. Complete the sentences with the correct verbs. Use the simple past tense.

leave spend take win sleep teach drive
buy pay speak fall meet ride make get

1. When my parents travelled in the Middle East, they _____ a camel.
2. Two years ago, John _____ a trip to Spain in a magazine contest.
3. When Christina was in Japan, she _____ English to school children for a year.
4. On their last trip to Greece, Carlos and Monica _____ all their money.
5. On his last business trip to Germany, Robert _____ German all the time.
6. The couple we _____ in Costa Rica last summer took hundreds of pictures.
7. Last summer, the children _____ late every morning.
8. Last winter, my brother _____ and broke his leg on a skiing trip.
9. Two years ago, we _____ all across the country in an old car.
10. The train to New York _____ late yesterday morning.
11. I _____ for the airline tickets with my credit card.
12. Our neighbours _____ dozens of souvenirs on their last trip to South America.
13. Jan and Bob _____ too much luggage when they went on vacation.
14. Frances _____ her daughter's cake by herself.
15. Jules and Suzanne _____ the last tickets before prices went up.

UNDERSTAND: **Simple Past Tense Negative Form**

Use the auxiliary verb **did + not** to show past time in the negative. Use the base form of the main verb. The contraction of **did not** is **didn't**.

> We **did not** like the restaurant last night.
> The plane **didn't** leave on time yesterday.

Language in Transition

Use the contraction in spoken English and informal written English. Use the full form in formal writing and for emphasis.

---

a kiosk a ticket booth a bus pass a token a pole					
	11	**12**	**13**	**14**	**15**

A. Change the verbs to the negative form. Use the contraction **didn't**.

1. Marianne liked to go to the beach when she was young.
2. Max spent time with his uncle in Brazil during the school year.
3. The airplane left on time because of the hurricane warning.
4. In the 1960s people needed visas to travel to the Soviet Union.
5. The diplomat received a warm welcome on his trip to France last week.
6. The tour guide took the children to the science museum this morning.
7. The diplomats stood in line with the other passengers at customs.
8. My brother ran in the Boston Marathon this year.
9. The agent asked for our boarding passes at the check-in counter.
10. We drank fresh fruit juice every time we went to the beach in Mexico.

UNDERSTAND: **Simple Past Tense Question Form**

Yes/No Questions

For yes/no questions in the simple past, use the auxiliary verb **did** before the subject. Use the base form of the main verb. For short answer replies to yes/no questions, use the subject and the auxiliary verb after **yes** or **no**.

Did you enjoy your last vacation? **Yes, I did.**

Did you go to the beach? **No, I didn't.**

A. Write yes/no questions that correspond to the following responses.

I arrived late at work this morning. **Did you arrive late?**

1. The employees demanded better working conditions.
2. Our neighbours invited us to come over for dinner.
3. The teacher asked the students why they were late.
4. Charles found learning Chinese very difficult.
5. They paid a lot of money for their airline tickets.
6. I waited a long time at the ticket counter.
7. Miriam broke her mother's favourite vase by accident.
8. Leo got malaria when he was travelling in the tropics.
9. The train accident occurred early yesterday morning.
10. He hurt himself while he was working on his car.

B. Write five yes/no questions to ask your partner. Ask each other the questions and practise giving short answers.

a ticket counter a schedule a timetable a waiting room an engine				
16	**17**	**18**	**19**	**20**

WH-Questions

For WH-information questions, put the WH-question word before the auxiliary verb **did**. Use the base form of the main verb.

 Where did you go on vacation last summer? I went to Toronto.

A. Work in pairs. Match the questions and answers.

1. How long did you wait at customs when you arrived in Paris?
2. How often did she travel when she was a teenager?
3. Where did they leave their dog while they were away?
4. When did their flight get in last night?
5. How on earth did she manage to lose her Visa card?
6. How long ago did those two artists meet?
7. Which group of students did Mr. Blake teach last session?
8. How much did she spend on redecorating her house?
9. How many hours did they stand in line to get tickets to the concert?
10. How did you feel after such a long flight?
11. Where exactly did the runner fall in the marathon?
12. Where did Lisa leave her new compact disk?
13. How much food did the passengers eat when the attendant brought the food trolley?
14. How much time did it take for the mechanic to repair the gearshift?
15. Where did you buy your bus pass?

a) I bought it at the ticket booth.
b) It took about two hours.
c) It got in at midnight.
d) They met only last year.
e) They left it at their neighbour's house.
f) I waited almost an hour.
g) They stood in line for about six hours.
h) She spent thousands of dollars.
i) I felt exhausted.
j) She doesn't know how she lost it.
k) She travelled with her family every summer.
l) He taught a group of business executives from Italy.
m) They ate almost all of it.
n) He fell just before the finish line.
o) She left it in the glove compartment.

a cabin a luggage rack a food trolley an aisle a cockpit					
	21	**22**	**23**	**24**	**25**

UNDERSTAND: **Present Perfect Aspect**

Aspect describes the relationship of two times. The present perfect aspect describes an action that began in the past and continues in the present.

> Janos has lived here for ten years. (and he still does)

The present perfect also describes an action that occurred at some unspecified time in the past and continues to have some relationship to present time.

> Have you visited New York? Yes, I have. (some time between the past and now)

To form the present perfect, use the auxiliary verb **have** (**has**) + the past participle of the main verb. Regular past participles are the same as the simple past form. Irregular past participles have to be learned by heart.

For a complete list of past tense and past participle forms see Appendix 2, page 190.

TEACHER'S BOX: The third person singular contraction for **have** is the same as the contraction for **be**. You can recognize the contraction of the present perfect by the use of the past participle after **he's**, **she's**, **it's**.

Present continuous: **he's going** (**he is** + present participle)
Present perfect: **he's gone** (**he has** + past participle)

A. Complete the sentences with the correct form of the present perfect.

1. My sister Karen _____ (be) in Switzerland for a while.
2. My grandparents _____ (live) for a long time.
3. The two pilots _____ (know) each other for years.
4. Those women _____ (be) friends for ages.
5. The association _____ (be) in existence for some time.
6. Hiroki _____ (speak) English most of his life.
7. Mr. Tan _____ (work) at the duty-free shop since he graduated.
8. Jackson _____ (go) to camp for three years now.
9. May _____ (lived) in this apartment as long as I have.
10. Annabel _____ (speak) French all her life.

TEACHER'S BOX: The present perfect for duration of time is used for a handful of commonly used verbs (**be, live, know, speak a language, work, go, have**). With most other verbs, the concept of duration of time is expressed with the present perfect continuous (see Unit 2).

---

a runway
a departure lounge
a departure gate
a duty-free shop
a conveyor belt

26   27   28   29   30

8

UNDERSTAND: **Simple Past Tense vs. Present Perfect Aspect**

1. Use the simple past for actions that began in the past and ended in the past at some specified or implied time. Use the present perfect aspect to describe actions that began in the past and continue in the present.

   Simple past: He lived in Rome for three years. (He doesn't live there anymore.)

   Present perfect: He has lived in Rome for three years. (He still does.)

A. Choose the simple past or the present perfect form of the verb.

1. The Smiths _____ (live) in the country for one year after they got married.

2. The roommates _____ (share) a room ever since they began university.

3. The two sales representatives _____ (work for) the same company for the past few months.

4. The dancers _____ (have) the same teacher since they started taking dancing lessons.

5. The researchers _____ (be) on the same team during the last research project.

6. The teacher _____ (know) the names of all the children in her kindergarten class.

7. The flight attendant _____ (work) for the same airline for the first three years of his career.

8. Those two politicians _____ (be) in opposing parties since they began their political careers.

9. Ted and Bob _____ (know) each other professionally for about a year now.

10. The musician _____ (have) an excellent piano teacher when he was young.

2. Use the simple past for actions that took place at some **specified** or implied time. Use the present perfect aspect to describe actions that took place at an **unspecified** time in the past.

   Simple past: Giovanni went to Russia in 1990.

   Present perfect: Giovanni has been to Russia. (at some time in the past)

a tray a flight attendant a screen a boarding pass luggage					
	31	32	33	34	35

B. Complete the story with the verbs indicated. Use the simple past tense or present perfect aspect.

My friend and I have decided that we want to study French in France. We both _____ (graduate) from college last month and we feel that this is an ideal time to do something interesting and productive before we start to work full time. I _____ (study) French for many years. My friend _____ (take) two courses in French at college last semester. However, she _____ (be) fascinated by the language for as long as I can remember.

Yesterday, we _____ (go) to several agencies and institutions to get information about different language schools in France. We _____ (spend) the whole day today trying to decide on the school and the city to go to. Finally, after many discussions and a few arguments, we _____ (choose) to go to Aix-en-Provence. Both my friend and I _____ (visit) Paris several times, but neither of us _____ (be) to Aix-en-Provence.

The only problem we have now is where to live. We _____ (decide) where to study, but we _____ (not decide) where to live. We _____ (hear) from different people that it is expensive to live in Aix-en-Provence and we cannot afford to stay too long. We _____ (save) a little money, but we need financial help from our parents too. This may be a problem because we _____ (not mention) our plans to our parents. This morning we _____ (discuss) our plans with our teacher and she recommended that we tell our parents about our plans right away.

C. Answer the questions about the paragraph above. Answer in complete sentences.

1. What have the two friends decided to do?
2. When did they graduate from college?
3. How long has the writer studied French?
4. How many French courses has her friend taken?
5. When did they go to find out about French courses?
6. How long did they spend trying to decide on a school?
7. Where did they finally choose to study?
8. How often have they visited Paris?
9. What have they not decided?
10. What have they heard about living in Aix-en-Provence?
11. How much money have they saved?
12. Why do they expect to have a problem with their parents?
13. What did they do in the morning?
14. What did she recommend?

a carousel
customs
baggage claim
a metal detector
a moving walkway

36   37   38   39   40

10

UNDERSTAND: **Present Perfect and Questions with "Ever"**

Use **ever** with the question form to indicate that you mean "at any time in the past." Do not use **ever** in affirmative statements.

> ✔ Have Hiroshi and Yoko ever been to New York?
>
> ✘ Hiroshi and Yoko have ever been to New York.

A. Choose the best words to complete the questions. Add **ever** to emphasize that you mean **at any time in the past**.

Have you _____ a kangaroo?　Have you **ever seen** a kangaroo?

visit　dream　see　attend　give　eat　fall　think　take　try

1. Have you _____ in the diner of a train?
2. Have they _____ the rainbow at Niagara Falls?
3. Has the teacher _____ a surprise examination?
4. Has anyone _____ a picture of the whole class?
5. Have you _____ to use a camera that didn't work?
6. Has Mario _____ a live baseball game?
7. Have your parents _____ your new apartment?
8. Has the weather here _____ below zero?
9. Has Susan _____ about switching fields of study?
10. Have you _____ of living in Hawaii?

UNDERSTAND: **Present Perfect and Negative with "Never"**

Use **never** with the present perfect to suggest "not at any time in the past." Put **never** between the auxiliary verb and the past participle of the main verb.

> I have **never** been to New York.

A. Complete the sentences with the present perfect form of the verb + **never**.

We _____ (see) so many people in the street.
We **have never seen** so many people in the street.

1. Jenna _____ (drive) in such a downpour.
2. I _____ (meet) so many people in one day.
3. Paco _____ (have) much self-confidence.

a coach car					
a diner					
a headrest					
a footrest					
a fold-out table	41	42	43	44	45

4. My aunt _____ (swim) in the ocean before.
5. Those students _____ (eat) real couscous.
6. Frances and Joe _____ (drink) beer, as far as I know.
7. Ziyad and Nadia _____ (meet) your parents.
8. That university _____ (give) courses in summer.
9. Mike _____ (lose) his temper with anyone at work.
10. That team _____ (win) a playoff game.

Vocabulary Challenge

Getting Around

Use the clues below to complete the puzzle.

Across

1. The train has been waiting on the _____ for ten minutes.
6. When the passengers checked in, their luggage was placed on the _____ .
9. A crowd of people went through the _____ on their way to the subway.
10. Several people were waiting at the _____ when the train pulled into the station.
11. The flight attendant helped some of the passengers put their bags in the overhead _____ .
12. To get to the subway, we had to follow a long passageway, and then go down the _____ .
14. Before they could board the international flight, all the passengers had to pass through the _____ .
17. Before I boarded the train, I went to the _____ to buy a newspaper and a snack.
18. I had to consult the _____ several times before I bought my train ticket.
19. The driver turned the _____ sharply to the left in order to avoid a stalled car in the right-hand lane.

Down

2. The plane was on the _____ , ready for take-off when the delay was announced.
3. Before she bought a ticket at the counter, the woman checked the _____ to see when the train departed.
4. The tired passenger rested his feet on the _____ in front of him, and had a nap.
5. Soon after the plane took off, each flight attendant took out a _____ and began to serve the food.
7. The passengers waited in the _____ until their flight was called.
8. After spending several hours in the plane, people began to walk up and down the _____ to stretch their legs.
13. The pilot and the co-pilot were in the _____ preparing for take-off.
15. Some of the train passengers went to the snack bar for lunch, but others went to the _____ for a hot meal.
16. The subway passengers had to hold on to the _____ as the train gained speed.
18. The young couple was happy that they had bought snow _____ when they travelled along icy side-roads last winter.

Ten-Minute Grammar Games

Do You Remember?

Focus: Review present perfect verbs.

Students make a list of 25 interesting or unusual activities they have done in their lives. The list should be written in the present perfect.

Examples: swum under a waterfall
got my first bicycle
ridden a horse
eaten snails

Then they put the items in one of the columns below.

I did it and I remember when	I have done it but I don't remember when	I started in the past and I am still doing it now

Participle Chain

Focus: Practise past participles.

Students work in pairs to make a chain of past participles. The last letter of each participle becomes the first letter of the next participle. They can see who can make the longest chain.

swum
    meant
        tried
            d...

Test Yourself

A. Cross out the incorrect forms on the list of past participles.

think	thought	~~thinked~~/thought
present	past	past participle

1. come — came — come/came
2. sit — sat — set/sat
3. choose — chose — chose/chosen
4. grow — grew — grown/grewn
5. ride — rode — rodden/ridden
6. feel — felt — felt/fallen
7. catch — caught — caught/catcht
8. draw — drew — drawn/drewn
9. forbid — forbade — forbidden/forbaden
10. shrink — shrank — shrunk/shrunken

B. Write questions that correspond to these answers, using appropriate WH-question words or phrases.

He bought three tickets.   How many tickets did he buy?

1. They went to China for their summer holidays last year.
2. Peter caught two salmon the last time he went fishing.
3. Gabriel felt sick during the long boat ride yesterday.
4. The students heard a lot of great classical music.
5. They camped in the forest on their last hiking trip.
6. The hotel receptionist woke us up at 7 o'clock.
7. I felt culture shock when I returned to North America.
8. They got sunburned because they didn't use sunscreen.
9. They drove a few hundred kilometres across the desert.
10. The football player had three accidents last season.

C. Choose the simple past or the present perfect form of the verb.

1. We _____ (take) a lot of photographs while we were on vacation.
2. The dog _____ (bite) three letter carriers since we moved here.
3. Po-Yee _____ (never buy) a lottery ticket in her life.
4. Everyone _____ (rise) to sing the national anthem before the game.
5. Scientists _____ (find) cures for many illnesses in the last 50 years.
6. _____ anyone here _____ (ever go) on an ocean cruise in the Caribbean?
7. Some of us _____ (go out) for dinner after the play last night.
8. One man _____ (forget) his camera when he left the airplane.
9. The spectators _____ (never see) such an exciting tennis match.
10. The boys _____ (catch) really bad colds when they went camping.

D. Find the errors and correct them. Check (✔) sentences that are correct.

1. We have ever seen the Empire State Building in New York.
2. Haven't you never tried to play tennis before?
3. The airline pilot has never flown a charter to Europe.
4. My friend hasn't never taken an airplane to Rome.
5. Has your family never visited the World Trade Centre?
6. They haven't never been to San Francisco in the spring.
7. Our friends have never heard of the CN Tower in Toronto.
8. Hasn't anyone here never ridden a horse before?
9. They haven't ever ridden on a ten-speed bicycle.
10. Have you ever eaten a dessert called Baked Alaska?

Score for Test Yourself: _____
40

Vocabulary Answers

1. windshield wipers	16. a waiting room	31. a screen
2. a glove compartment	17. a timetable	32. a boarding pass
3. a gearshift	18. an engine	33. a flight attendant
4. tires	19. a ticket counter	34. luggage
5. a steering wheel	20. a schedule	35. a tray
6. tracks	21. an aisle	36. customs
7. a platform edge	22. a cabin	37. a moving walkway
8. a turnstile	23. a luggage rack	38. a carousel
9. a fare box	24. a cockpit	39. a metal detector
10. an escalator	25. a food trolley	40. baggage claim
11. a token	26. a duty-free shop	41. a footrest
12. a bus pass	27. a runway	42. a diner
13. a pole	28. a conveyor belt	43. a headrest
14. a kiosk	29. a departure lounge	44. a fold-out table
15. a ticket booth	30. a departure gate	45. a coach car

Present Perfect Continuous

What Do You Know?

How Long Has This Been Going On?

Think of things you have been doing for five of the following periods of time. Then compare your list with a partner.

for six months I have been studying English.

for three years _____

for six months _____

for ten years _____

for three weeks _____

for two months _____

for five years _____

for two years _____

for two days _____

since last week _____

since January _____

for eight years _____

Understanding Grammar

UNDERSTAND: **Present Perfect Continuous**

Use of Present Perfect Continuous

The present perfect continuous aspect describes an action that began in the past, is progressive, and is still continuing in the present.

> My neighbour has been playing the tuba all afternoon.
>
> (He began to play it earlier, has played it continuously, and is still playing it now.)

Both stative (non-action) and dynamic (action) verbs can have perfective aspect, but only dynamic verbs can have continuous aspect. Therefore, stative verbs cannot be expressed in the present perfect continuous form.

> ✔ I have liked armchairs since I was young.
>
> ✘ I have been liking armchairs since I was young.

See Appendix 3, page 192 for a list of common stative verbs.

TEACHER'S BOX: Some verbs are stative in their basic meaning but also have colloquial meanings in which they are dynamic.

> ✘ I have been seeing a book on the table.   ✔ Janet has been seeing Mike romantically.
>
> ✘ I have been having a car.   ✔ I have been having fun.

A. Look at the list of expressions and find the ones with dynamic verbs.

1. wait for someone
2. have a car
3. believe that story
4. meet someone
5. know someone
6. have a good time
7. see a special boyfriend
8. hear good things about you
9. see a tiger
10. live in Vancouver
11. be president
12. study for an exam
13. eat a hamburger
14. have a sister
15. know my name
16. speak Turkish
17. work for the government
18. hear good news
19. have a bath
20. like my brother

curtains blinds drapes a ceiling fan a chandelier					
	1	2	3	4	5

Form of Present Perfect Continuous

When you form the present perfect continuous, there are two aspects involved, the perfective aspect and the continuous aspect. The perfective aspect suggests that two times (past and present) are involved. You express the perfective aspect first by using **have** + the past participle of **be** (been).

> She has been…

You express the continuous aspect second by using the present participle of the main verb.

> She **has been studying** English since high school.

A. Write sentences in the present perfect continuous form using the dynamic (action) verbs from the list on page 18. Use a separate sheet of paper.

> wait for someone   I have been waiting for you for an hour.

UNDERSTAND: **Additional Uses of the Present Perfect Continuous**

Actions Finished in Immediate Past Time

One common use of the present perfect continuous is to show that an action finished in the immediate past. The present perfect continuous describes an action that was completed just before the moment of speaking. In other words, the action is completed, but the result of the action can still be seen in the present. Note that, in contrast, the present perfect aspect describes an action that was completed at an unspecified time in the past.

> They have painted the living room.
> (Present perfect: It is a different colour but we don't know when they painted it.)

> They have been painting the living room.
> (Present perfect continuous: We know it just happened because we can see the cans of paint and the ladder.)

a night table a coffee table an end table a floor lamp an armchair					
	6	7	8	9	10

20

A. Look at the pictures and answer the questions. Answer with full sentences.

1. What has she been doing?
2. What has he been doing?
3. What have they been doing?
4. What has he been doing?
5. What has she been doing?
6. What have they been doing?
7. What has she been doing?
8. What has he been doing?
9. What have they been doing?
10. What have they been doing?

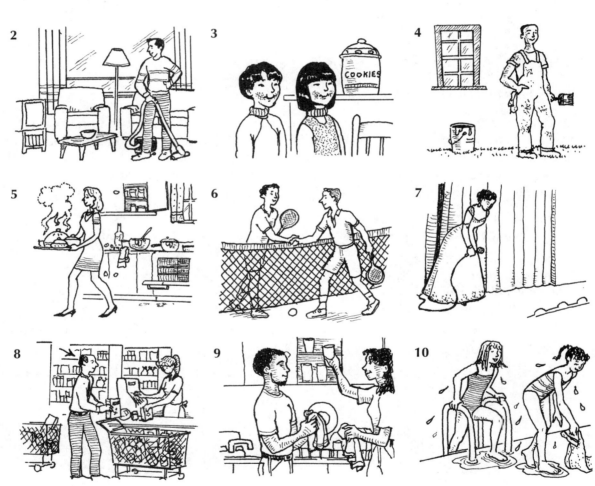

a bottle opener a can opener a corkscrew a ladle a grater					
	11	**12**	**13**	**14**	**15**

B. Match the situation with the question you would ask.

The little boy is dirty. Has he been playing in the mud?

1. There is a delicious smell coming from the kitchen.
2. Did you see how red and tired Dan's eyes look?
3. I noticed several books on your night table.
4. That blond nurse looks absolutely exhausted.
5. The house is immaculate; it's really clean.
6. Pedro's English is much better than it used to be.
7. Your clothes are soaking wet!
8. I have a lot of bags and packages.
9. Those two men can't walk a straight line.
10. Elena looks much slimmer than last time I saw her.

a) Have they been drinking too much?
b) Have you been walking in the rain?
c) Have you been shopping all day?
d) Has she been dieting?
e) Have they been spring cleaning?
f) Has he been playing too many computer games?
g) Has he been studying harder than usual?
h) Have you been reading late at night?
i) Has she been working an extra shift?
j) Has someone been baking cookies?

Recent Habits or Unusual Behaviour

Another use of the present perfect continuous is to describe recent habits or new, unusual behaviour. Time markers such as **recently** and **lately** are generally used to show that the habits described are new ones.

> **Usually** Tom goes to bed early. **Lately**, he has been staying up until midnight.

> She has been making a lot of milkshakes in her blender **recently**.
> (Normally, she doesn't make milkshakes.)

a blender a toaster a microwave a freezer a food processor					
	16	17	18	19	20

A. Give reasons for the situations that are explained here. Use the information in brackets to write affirmative or negative sentences using the present perfect continuous. Add words such as **lately** and **recently**.

Mike has gained 5 kilos. (eat too much spaghetti)
He has been eating too much spaghetti recently.

Valerie looks exhausted all the time. (not get enough sleep)
She hasn't been getting enough sleep lately.

1. The baseball team has lost a lot of games. (not play well)
2. John has developed large muscles. (exercise a lot)
3. Yumiko's pronunciation has improved tremendously. (practise in the lab)
4. It takes us less time to prepare supper these days. (use a microwave)
5. The kids are doing better in school. (not watch so much TV)
6. David looks really different these days. (grow a beard)
7. Mike seems to have a lot of money. (work at two jobs)
8. Something must be wrong with our toaster. (burning everything)
9. I think I must be catching a cold. (sneeze a lot)
10. Mario's English isn't improving. (not study much)

B. Work with a partner asking and answering these questions. Before you begin, write three questions of your own using the present perfect continuous.

Have you been working too hard lately?   Yes, I have.
                                       No, I haven't.

1. _____?
2. _____?
3. _____?
4. Have you been studying a lot this week?
5. Have you been doing your homework this term?
6. Have you been practising English on the weekends?
7. Have you been speaking your own language more than English?
8. Have you been eating well lately?
9. Have you been getting enough exercise?
10. Have you been watching a lot of TV recently?

a pillow					
a blanket					
sheets					
a quilt					
a comforter					
	21	22	23	24	25

UNDERSTAND: **Present Perfect Continuous Negative Form**

Use **not** after the auxiliary verb **have** to make the negative form of the present perfect continuous.

He has **not** been eating much lately.

A. Match the comments with the explanations.

1. Stephen has had a backache for the last three days.
2. The students' apartment is in a really big mess.
3. Tina is hanging her sheets on the clothes line.
4. Janet has felt really tired all morning.
5. The neighbours' lawn is turning yellow.
6. Sam has been late for work three days in a row.
7. The new parents are looking exhausted.
8. The teacher is looking frustrated.
9. People on the street have been slipping on the ice.
10. Pat and Tom are looking much slimmer.

a) She hasn't been getting enough sleep lately.
b) He hasn't been setting his alarm clock.
c) The city hasn't been cleaning the sidewalks.
d) They haven't been cleaning it regularly.
e) He hasn't been sleeping on a firm mattress.
f) Her students haven't been paying attention.
g) Her dryer hasn't been working lately.
h) They haven't been eating desserts lately.
i) They haven't been watering it regularly.
j) The baby hasn't been sleeping through the night.

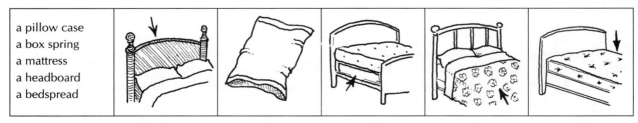

a pillow case					
a box spring					
a mattress					
a headboard					
a bedspread	26	27	28	29	30

Vocabulary Challenge

Around the House

Put these words into categories. You should have five groups of three words each.

> **toaster   can opener   mattress   sheets   blender   drapes   corkscrew   box spring
> pillows   blankets   blinds   bottle opener   curtains   headboard   microwave**

Ten-Minute Grammar Games

Find Someone

Focus: Practise present perfect continuous.

The aim is for students to find at least one person who fits each description on the list. Students walk around the room asking each other questions. When a person answers "Yes," his or her name is written beside the description on the list. The first person to finish is the winner. Students in the class can be asked to confirm or deny the information as the winner reads it out.

Find someone who…
1. has been taking the bus to class
2. has been smoking for at least three years
3. hasn't been reading the newspaper regularly lately
4. hasn't been doing his or her homework regularly this month
5. hasn't been cooking meals regularly since the course began
6. has been watching a lot of movies on TV lately
7. has been listening to music on a walkman on the way to class recently
8. has been bringing his or her lunch to work or class every day
9. has been coming to class late a lot recently
10. has been wearing blue jeans to class every day recently

Is It True?

Focus: Practise present perfect continuous.

This activity can be done with the whole class or in groups.

Each student writes down an unusual activity about himself or herself, using the present perfect continuous. The activity can be real or imaginary.

> I've been taking care of five cats for my neighbours who are on vacation.
> I've been studying Latin.

A student reads his or her list aloud. Other students try to work out if the statement is true or false by asking questions. The student answering the questions should try to make it as difficult as possible for the others to guess. The student who guesses reads his or her statement next, and the game continues.

Test Yourself

A. Write these sentences using the present perfect continuous form of the verb.

1. John is managing an all-night gas station.
2. Suzanne is training for the Olympic Games.
3. Maria is teaching swimming at the YWCA.
4. Lili and Chen are renting an apartment downtown.
5. Max and Bob are building a boat in the basement.
6. The government is trying to discourage smoking.
7. Our school is offering scholarships to good students.
8. My grandmother is baking cookies for the bazaar on Saturday.
9. Julia is taking a French course this summer.
10. Marta is sewing a dress for her younger sister.

B. Complete the dialogue with the simple past, present perfect, or present perfect continuous form of the verb in brackets.

Nancy: Hi Keiko! How are things? I _____ (not see) you for a long time.

Keiko: Hi Nancy! Things are going great. How are you?

Nancy: I'm OK, but I _____ (be) really busy with school and my new job. I finally _____ (graduate) last December. How about you? _____ (you finish) your management certificate yet?

Keiko: Oh yes, I _____ (get) my diploma last spring. I _____ (look) for a job for the past couple of months.

Nancy: _____ (you have) any luck so far?

Keiko: So far, I _____ (have) a few interviews, but no job offers yet. What _____ (you do) since you finished school?

Nancy: I _____ (not find) the job I want yet either, but I _____ (work) part-time, so I am not too worried.

Keiko: Where _____ (you work)?

Nancy: At the same law firm where I _____ (work) last summer.

Keiko: That's good! Do you see any of the people we used to hang around with?

Nancy: Not really, except for Carlos Rodriguez. Do you remember him?

Keiko: Sure. What _____ (he do) since the last time we saw him?

Nancy: He _____ (work) for American Airlines. We _____ (go out) together for about six months now. Are you seeing anyone?

Keiko: I guess we really _____ (not talk) for a long time. I'm engaged to be married.

Nancy: Really! To whom?

Keiko: Tom Walker. We _____ (be) engaged for a year and we're getting married next spring.

Nancy: That's fantastic. Congratulations!

Keiko: Thanks. Well, I have to run. I _____ (miss) two buses already. But let's stay in touch. Here's my phone number.

Nancy: And here's mine. It _____ (be) great seeing you again.

C. Complete the explanations with the correct form of the present perfect continuous (affirmative or negative). Match the situations and the explanations.

1. Rocco has failed two science exams this week.
2. Mei-Ling fell asleep in philosophy class today.
3. Frederick has been late for class three times this week.
4. The teacher looks angry when she comes to class.
5. Mica had excellent marks in chemistry this term.
6. Keiko runs to the mailbox as soon as the mail comes.
7. Natasha doesn't look as homesick as she used to.
8. The classroom looks dirtier than usual today.
9. The food in the cafeteria was really tasty yesterday.
10. Miguel left class earlier than usual today.

a) The cook _____ (get) better all the time.
b) She _____ (study) in the library every day.
c) She _____ (not miss) her parents as much as before.
d) She _____ (go to bed) after midnight recently.
e) Her students _____ (not do) their assignments on time.
f) The janitor _____ (not clean) very conscientiously lately.
g) He _____ (not study) as much as he should lately.
h) He _____ (go) to the doctor for some treatment.
i) She _____ (expect) an important letter from home.
j) He _____ (not set) his alarm clock properly.

Score for Test Yourself: _____
40

Vocabulary Answers

1. blinds	11. a can opener	21. a blanket
2. a chandelier	12. a corkscrew	22. a pillow
3. a ceiling fan	13. a grater	23. a comforter
4. curtains	14. a ladle	24. sheets
5. drapes	15. a bottle opener	25. a quilt
6. an armchair	16. a toaster	26. a headboard
7. a coffee table	17. a freezer	27. a pillowcase
8. a night table	18. a blender	28. a box spring
9. an end table	19. a microwave	29. a bedspread
10. a floor lamp	20. a food processor	30. a mattress

<table>
<tr><td>

3

</td><td>

Gerunds as Subjects, Objects, and Complements
Gerunds vs. Infinitives
"Make/Let someone do something"

</td></tr>
</table>

What Do You Know?

What—Me Do That?

Put the activities on the list below into categories according to your feelings about them. Use the chart on page 28. Add five of your own activities to the list.

fishing
biking
camping
shopping
taking pictures
babysitting
cooking
washing the dishes
playing the piano
hiking
sailing
singing
watching TV
reading
walking a dog
building a fire
using tools
driving a car
swimming
travelling by bus
going to movies alone
ice skating

riding a horse
riding a bicycle
surfing
writing letters
studying
speaking another language
playing the guitar
ironing clothes
eating fast food
meeting new people
owning a pet
travelling abroad
taking a plane
being late for work
playing computer games
renting a car
feeding a cat
doing homework
talking on the phone
taking medicine
seeing the dentist
in-line skating

28

Love to do/Love doing	Can tolerate doing	Hate to do/Hate doing

a tennis racket
a badminton
 racket
squash
a net
a hoop

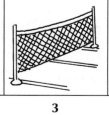

1   2   3   4   5

Understanding Grammar

UNDERSTAND: **Gerunds as Subjects, Objects, and Complements**

A gerund is the present participle form of the verb that functions as a noun in a sentence. To form a gerund, add **ing** to the base form of the verb.

I eat every day.   **Eating** is necessary.
I jog to work.   I enjoy **jogging**.

Just like a noun, a gerund can be used as the subject, object, complement, or object of a preposition in a sentence.

Subject: **Jogging** can be good for your health.
Object: A lot of athletes enjoy **jogging**.
Complement: His favourite exercise is **jogging**.
Object of a preposition: You need special shoes for **jogging**.

A. Use a gerund to replace the words in bold type. Make necessary changes.

Cigarettes are harmful to your health.
Smoking is harmful to your health.

1. **Books** can help you pass many happy hours.
2. **Lies** always get people into trouble.
3. That student wants to continue **his studies** for a Ph.D.
4. The doctor suggested **exercise** as a way to relieve stress.
5. **Our visit** to Australia was a great experience.
6. I saw lots of **tears** at the goodbye ceremony.
7. He enjoyed **his trips** to Asia when he was young.
8. The old couple used to like **to take walks** in the park.
9. **Jokes** are a good way to relieve tension.
10. People from many cultures find folk **dances** enjoyable.
11. **Preparations** for holidays are part of the fun.
12. He enjoyed **his rest** after a long and tiring day.

golf clubs a tee a baseball bat a mitt a baseball diamond					
	6	7	8	9	10

B. Underline the gerunds. Replace the gerunds with appropriate nouns from the list below.

<u>Exercising</u> daily is a good way to keep fit. **aerobics**

**insomnia   a fax   agitation   books and magazines   trips   urban life
a strict diet   stamp collections   language study   summer jobs**

1. Travelling to other countries can be an exciting experience.
2. Both children and adults like collecting stamps.
3. Reading can be both educational and entertaining.
4. Taking language courses abroad is an increasingly popular activity.
5. Living in a big city can be either stressful or exciting.
6. Sending instant correspondence is a good way to conduct business.
7. Students in North America like working during the holidays to make money.
8. Having difficulty sleeping can lead to exhaustion and irritability.
9. Obsessive dieting is not always the best way to lose weight.
10. Twitching and shaking can be a sign of unbearable stress.

UNDERSTAND: **Gerunds as Subjects and Objects**

Gerunds can be used in place of nouns as the subject or object in a sentence.

    Subject: **Swimming** is good for the health.
    Object: Doctors recommend **swimming** regularly.

A. Complete the sentence with the appropriate verb from the list below. Use the gerund form.

Doctors warn that **smoking** is bad for your health.

take   wear   dive   play   exercise   travel   learn   watch   relax   postpone

1. Most people know that _____ a helmet protects your head from injury.
2. _____ daily can help you to stay in good physical shape.
3. People who are interested in other cultures enjoy _____.
4. People who are workaholics generally don't like _____.
5. _____ from a high board can be a thrilling experience.
6. _____ a chair-lift is a quick way to get to the top of a mountain.
7. When you study a new language, _____ vocabulary is important.
8. People who procrastinate always try _____ jobs till later.
9. _____ horror films before you go to bed causes nightmares.
10. Tennis players avoid _____ tennis outdoors when the weather is bad.

a coach a stroke a bathing cap a diving board a trampoline					
	11	**12**	**13**	**14**	**15**

UNDERSTAND: **Gerunds as Complements**

The gerund form can be used to complete an idea after the verb **be**.

A popular winter activity **is skiing**.

A. Complete the sentences. Use the verbs below in the gerund form.

overeat skate wait join save carry ski camp sleep swim

1. The best way to meet new people is _____ organizations.
2. One of the most expensive sports is _____.
3. A vital concern of environmentalists is _____ the rain forest.
4. One thing golfers don't like is _____ their clubs around all day.
5. An activity our next door neighbours enjoy in the summer is _____ in the National Park.
6. The activity I like best on a winter day is _____.
7. One thing that makes people gain weight is _____.
8. When we are at the beach, our favorite activity is _____.
9. One thing most skiers don't like is _____ for the chair-lift.
10. One thing Mary enjoys on a Saturday morning is _____.

UNDERSTAND: **Gerunds as Objects of Prepositions**

Use the gerund form of the verb following a preposition.

I worry **about** losing my car keys.

A. Choose the correct prepositions. If you need help, see page 39.

1. He is interested (by / in) taking a course in either aikido or karate.
2. Some children are afraid (of / about) sleeping alone in the dark.
3. A lot of people don't approve (for / of) testing cosmetic products on animals.
4. Many baseball fans look forward (to / at) listening to games on the radio.
5. The outcome of the game depends (of / on) scoring goals.
6. When they saw the storm, the travellers decided (for / on) waiting until morning.
7. The politician apologized (about / for) making an offensive comment during his speech.
8. The success of any project depends (of / on) careful planning at the outset.
9. The people on the tour became fed up (with / by) eating in restaurants every night.
10. The swimmers complained (about / from) wearing bathing caps when they swam in the pool.

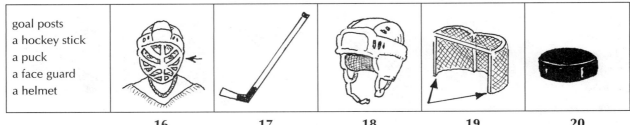

goal posts a hockey stick a puck a face guard a helmet				
16	**17**	**18**	**19**	**20**

11. The committee thanked the participants (with/by) giving them each a small gift.
12. Most of the people who took the tennis course last week seemed to be pretty good (for/at) getting the ball over the net.
13. Some of the players didn't agree (about/with) cancelling the game.
14. After what they had done for me, I thanked them all heartily (for/of) helping me out.
15. Not everybody believes (in/for) going swimming as the best form of exercise.

Some verbs are associated with certain prepositions but require a direct object before the preposition.

The government **warned** people **against smoking**.

Verbs	+ Direct Object	+ Preposition
warn	someone	against
thank	someone	for
prevent	someone	from
suspect	someone	of
accuse	someone	of
congratulate	someone	on
stop	someone	from
forgive	someone	for
advise	someone	against

B. Choose the best verb to complete the sentences. Use the gerund form of the verb.

Jan **accused** Tim **of laughing** at her accent.

cheat   forget   speed   win   help   copy   fall   smoke   invest   leave

1. Mary thanked her swimming coach for _____ her with her stroke.
2. Sylvia's aunt congratulated her on _____ the game.
3. The police advised motorists against _____ on city streets.
4. The woman forgave her son for _____ to mail the letter.
5. The captain accused the other team of _____ in the final game.
6. The boss advised us against _____ early on Friday afternoon.
7. Joe's financial advisor warned him against _____ in that company.
8. The railing prevented people from _____ over the cliff.
9. The doctor warned him about _____ when he developed a cough.
10. An invigilator accused a student of _____ another student's answers.

skis a chair-lift ski poles bindings a slope				
21	**22**	**23**	**24**	**25**

Didacthèque Carmen-Lachance
Département des sciences de l'éducation
Université du Québec à Hull

33

UNDERSTAND: **Gerunds vs. Infinitives**

When one verb follows another in a sentence, the second verb has either a gerund form or an infinitive form. Some verbs are followed by gerunds, some verbs are followed by infinitives, and some verbs can be followed by either a gerund or an infinitive.

✘ They enjoy to skate. (infinitive)

✔ He forgot to water the plants. (infinitive)

✔ She likes to dance. (infinitive)

✔ They enjoy skating. (gerund)

✘ He forgot watering the plants. (gerund)

✔ She likes dancing. (gerund)

Verbs and Expressions Followed by the Gerund

admit advise anticipate appreciate avoid consider delay deny discuss dislike dread enjoy escape excuse finish forgive imagine involve keep know like mention mind miss postpone practise quit recommend regret resent resist risk stop suggest tolerate understand

I can't help	it involves	there's no point
I don't mind	keep on	to have difficulty
it's not worth	never mind	to have trouble

Verbs and Expressions Followed by the Infinitive

agree appear arrange ask attempt beg can't wait care choose claim consent dare decide demand deserve expect fail forget happen hesitate hope intend learn manage mean neglect need offer prepare plan pledge promise resolve seem struggle swear tend threaten want wish

can't afford
I am determined

Verbs and Expressions Followed by Either Gerund or Infinitive

begin can't bear can't stand continue hate like love neglect prefer propose remember start try

it's a waste of money
it's a waste of time

---

archery					
a target					
a bull's eye					
a running track					
a finish line					
	26	27	28	29	30

> **TEACHER'S BOX:** Many recreational activities are expressed by using the verb **go** followed by the gerund: **go swimming, go dancing, go shopping, go sightseeing, go bowling, go camping,** etc.

A. Circle the correct form of the verb in each sentence. If both forms are possible circle both of them.

1. The bad-tempered gourmet chef refused (making/to make) a hamburger for the American tourist.
2. The arrogant actress demanded (having/to have) champagne with every meal.
3. The eternal optimist tried (getting/to get) a job interview with the company that had refused him three times.
4. The great procrastinator managed (finishing/to finish) his project just in time.
5. The overzealous runner decided (entering/to enter) the marathon before he was in shape.
6. The movie fanatic admitted (spending/to spend) every evening at the movie theatre.
7. The absent-minded professor forgot (giving/to give) his history course on Wednesday.
8. The eccentric artist chose (walking around/to walk around) with his cat on a leash.
9. The vain model enjoyed (looking/to look) at herself in the mirror every chance she got.
10. The self-conscious speaker practised (giving/to give) his speech for a whole week.
11. The dishonest accountant denied (changing/to change) the figures on the balance sheet.
12. The spoiled child grew up expecting (having/to have) everything he wanted.
13. The newly-converted vegetarian wouldn't stop (telling/to tell) everyone how unhealthy it was to eat meat.
14. The self-centred passenger liked (taking/to take) two seats in the crowded bus.
15. The hungry teenager began (eating/to eat) as soon as she got home from school.

B. Choose the best verb to complete the sentence. Put it in the present simple or simple past tense according to the context.

dislike   claim   arrange   postpone   mind   offer   fail   risk   involve   admit

1. I don't _____ people smoking in the same building, but I object if they are in the same room.
2. We _____ leaving for our trip, but we forgot to change our tickets.
3. At the police station the thief _____ stealing the money, but he apologized to the people he had robbed.
4. The teacher _____ to repeat the lesson, but the students told her that it wasn't necessary.

a court a rink ice skates blades in-line skates					
	31	32	33	34	35

5. The tennis player _____ to pick up his racket at the shop at 3:00, but it wasn't ready.
6. People who go sailing during a heavy storm _____ drowning in the heavy seas.
7. The writer _____ hearing any criticism of the characters in her novels.
8. The basketball player _____ to put the ball through the hoop, and lost the game.
9. The champion archer _____ to be able to hit the bull's eye, but he missed.
10. Being in good physical and mental condition _____ doing a lot of exercise on a regular basis.

C. Complete the following sentences using gerunds or infinitives.

1. The crooked politician claimed (not know) _____ the strategies of the other party.
2. My English teacher recommends (use) _____ a dictionary to check on unfamiliar vocabulary.
3. When we play tennis in hot weather, we should avoid (stay) _____ out in the sun at high noon for too long.
4. Honest people deserve (be) _____ trusted in business and personal relationships.
5. The dance lover proposed (do) _____ the tango at the dance contest.
6. The underpaid workers demanded (have) _____ a raise after working for six months.
7. Insecure people often hesitate (speak up) _____ in meetings or in large groups.
8. Active children hate (go) _____ to bed early when it is still light.
9. All the witnesses swore (tell) _____ the truth during the long trial.
10. All the chess players practised (check) _____ their opponents before the big tournament began.

UNDERSTAND: **"Make/Let someone do something"**

Make and **let** are two verbs that are followed by the base form of the main verb. **Make** means to cause, force, compel, or pressure someone to do something. **Let** means to allow something or give permission to someone to do something. **Make** and **let** can be used in the past, present, or future forms. The negative form is made with the auxiliary verb **do**.

My mother **made me wash** the dishes yesterday.
My mother **doesn't let me stay up** late on week days.
The teacher **will make us hand in** our homework before class.

The verbs **make** and **let** are always followed by an object + the base form of the main verb.

The parents made **the children go** to bed early.
My friend didn't let **me use** his brand new car.

A. Rewrite the following sentences using **make** or **let**. Make necessary changes.

1. The doctor doesn't allow anyone to smoke in the waiting room.
2. The story was very sad and it caused me to cry.
3. We do not allow our children to stay up after 8:00.
4. The police forced the thief to return the stolen money.
5. The boss pressured all the workers to do overtime.
6. The teacher gave us permission to hand in our assignments late.
7. The parents allowed their teenager to drive their car only on the weekends.
8. Weather conditions forced us to change our holiday plans.
9. The spoiled fish that we ate at dinner caused everyone to be sick.
10. The pool supervisor doesn't allow children to use the pool unsupervised.

Vocabulary Challenge

What Could It Be?

Put the missing words from each sentence into the puzzle. Then find the hidden words.

1. People jump off _____ and plunge into the water.
2. Passing the _____ takes quick reflexes in a hockey game.
3. Throwing the most balls through a _____ is the way to win at basketball.

4. If we didn't have _____ , we would be spending a lot of time climbing ski hills.
5. Wearing a _____ keeps your hair dry when you swim.
6. Using _____ helps us keep our balance when we ski.
7. To begin playing golf, put your ball on a _____ .
8. Playing _____ involves hitting a ball with a racket in an indoor court.
9. If you want to win at archery, you should be shooting for the _____ .
10. Wearing a _____ protects your hands when you catch a hard ball.
11. The key to scoring in hockey is shooting the puck between the _____ .
12. People enjoy playing _____ with rackets and a bird.
13. Wearing a _____ protects your head when you play contact sports.
14. If you like jumping, try a _____ .
15. Playing basketball or squash is usually done on a _____ .

Ten-Minute Grammar Games

Sentence Ends

Focus: Practise completing sentences using gerunds and infinitives.

Students complete these sentences alone. They should use gerunds or infinitives. Then they work in groups to talk about their answers. They can ask each other questions to find out more.

> I can't stand watching hockey on TV.
> I'm fond of visiting my aunt and uncle.

1. I am interested in…
2. I have difficulty with…
3. I admit…
4. I plan…
5. I don't mind…
6. I look forward to…
7. It's a waste of money…
8. I'm fed up with…
9. I can't stand…
10. I insist on…
11. I regret…
12. I'm anxious about…
13. I can't wait…
14. I'm determined…

An Activity Survey

Focus: Practise questions and answers using gerunds and infinitives.

Students work in groups. They brainstorm a list of ten activities they would like to ask about, and write questions using the gerund or infinitive form.

> What are some sports you enjoy playing?
> How much time do you spend watching TV every day?

Then they survey four other students in the class. They ask the questions they have prepared and get as much information as they can for each one.

They meet back in their groups to compare information. Then they prepare a class profile to present to the class.

Test Yourself

A. Replace the words in bold with gerunds that mean the same thing.

Chess is a satisfying hobby to have. Playing chess…

**growing up   living   switching jobs   improving his diet   waiting
writing   working   travelling   staying   watching TV**

1. John is considering **a job with that company**.
2. I can't stand **long line-ups** when I go to see a movie.
3. She started **her journal** when she was only six years old.
4. We considered **a house** in the country but it was too far from work.
5. She didn't like working in offices, so she tried **to get other jobs**.
6. The doctor advised him about **better eating habits**.
7. **Television programs** with violence can upset young children.
8. She doesn't remember **her youth** in Spain very well.
9. They found **the hotel** at the seashore very comfortable.
10. **The trip they made** to South America was very interesting.

B. Fill in the correct prepositions.

1. He is afraid _____ meeting a boa constrictor in the jungle.
2. They are not keen _____ taking too many courses in summer.
3. My friend Max is very good _____ doing manual tasks.
4. Most children are pretty fond _____ their grandparents.
5. Active people are usually enthusiastic _____ outdoor sports.
6. Some of my friends are really bad _____ keeping secrets.
7. Parents sometimes become too worried _____ their children.
8. Many people were interested _____ taking that course.
9. After reading the brochure we decided _____ going there.
10. The politician couldn't agree _____ anything on the agenda.

C. Complete the sentences with the gerund or the infinitive form of the verb.

1. The tourists considered _____ (go) to the beach in the morning rather than the afternoon.
2. Night owls are people who don't enjoy _____ (get up) early in the morning.
3. Some men dislike _____ (wear) ties, even on formal occasions such as weddings.
4. Certain people never dare _____ (take) risks in case they have a bad experience.
5. The speaker appeared _____ (be) very calm, but inside he was quite nervous.
6. After much discussion, Mario consented _____ (drive) the younger children to the birthday party.

7. Workaholics are people who usually can't wait _____ (go) back to work after a holiday.

8. The unemployed man struggled _____ (support) his wife and children by doing odd jobs.

9. The sprinters practised _____ (leave) the starting blocks as quickly as possible.

10. The coach suggested _____ (meet) for dinner when practice was over.

D. Some sentences have errors. Find the errors and correct them. Check (✔) correct sentences.

1. Josephine's mother didn't let her to play outside after dark.

2. The piano teacher makes the students to practise every day.

3. The museum guards did not let the tourists photographing the famous paintings.

4. The police made the neighbours turn down the music.

5. The news of the happy event made everyone feel more cheerful.

6. The usher made everyone who arrived late waited until the intermission.

7. The teacher let the students bringing coffee to class.

8. The computer teacher will let you use the terminals on weekends.

9. The teacher always makes her students memorizing irregular verbs.

10. The speaker will let everyone ask questions after the lecture.

Score for Test Yourself: _____
                          40

Help for Exercise A, page 31

Verbs and Adjectives Followed by Preposition + Gerund

agree on	dream of
apologize for	insist on
approve of	look forward to
decide against	succeed in
depend on	think about
disapprove of	think of
be afraid of	be good at
be anxious about	be interested in
be bored with	be keen on
be enthusiastic about	be tired of
be fed up with	be worried about
be fond of	

Vocabulary Answers

1. a hoop	13. a stroke	25. ski poles
2. a tennis racket	14. a coach	26. a finish line
3. a net	15. a bathing cap	27. a running track
4. a badminton racket	16. a face guard	28. archery
5. squash	17. a hockey stick	29. a bull's eye
6. a baseball bat	18. a helmet	30. a target
7. a tee	19. goal posts	31. blades
8. a mitt	20. a puck	32. in-line skates
9. a baseball diamond	21. bindings	33. a court
10. golf clubs	22. skis	34. ice skates
11. a trampoline	23. a slope	35. a rink
12. a diving board	24. a chair-lift	

4 Tag Questions

Expressions: "I do too." "So do I."
"I don't either." "Neither do I."

What Do You Know?

Agree or Disagree?

Comment on the statements saying whether you agree or disagree. Use one of the short answer forms below.

Agree	Disagree
I do too. So do I.	I don't.
I don't either. Neither do I.	I do.

1. I usually eat a midnight snack.
2. I sometimes ride a mountain-bike in the summer.
3. I often play electronic games.
4. I like listening to Italian opera.
5. I never forget to use the flash when I take pictures.
6. I often go bowling on Saturday night.
7. I never arrive late for work or class.
8. I sometimes arrive late for work or class.
9. I like to scuba-dive in the ocean.
10. I enjoy mountain-climbing in a group.
11. I don't like to water-ski.
12. I seldom watch curling on TV.
13. I enjoy playing chess on winter nights.

14. I prefer cross-country skiing to downhill skiing.
15. I like to skateboard when the weather is fine.
16. I never go ice-fishing.
17. I enjoy gardening in the summer.
18. I spend a lot of time listening to classical music.
19. I don't like listening to rock music.
20. I never go bird-watching.

Understanding Grammar

UNDERSTAND: **Tag Questions**

A tag question is a short expression that is used at the end of a sentence for one of two reasons: to seek confirmation or agreement, or to ask for information.

Tag Questions to Seek Confirmation or Agreement

Use a tag question when you already know the answer and are asking the other person to confirm your opinion or to agree with the statement you have made.

> It's a beautiful day, isn't it? (The answer expected is, "Yes it is.")
>
> It wasn't too hard, was it? (The answer expected is, "No it wasn't.")

Use falling intonation with the tag question to signal that you are expecting agreement from the other person. Falling intonation means that the voice goes down at the end of the sentence.

> It's a beautiful day, isn't it?

Tag Questions to Ask for Information

Use a tag question to ask a question to which you don't know the answer. The answer may be either "Yes" or "No," depending on the information in the response.

> You haven't paid the bill, have you?
>
> Possible answers: Yes, I have.
>
>   No, I haven't.

Use rising intonation to signal that you are requesting information from the other person. Rising intonation means that the voice goes up at the end of the sentence.

> You haven't paid the bill, have you?

windsurfing surfing mountain-biking scuba-diving water-skiing					
	1	2	3	4	5

To form a tag question, use the auxiliary verb from the main statement (**be**, **have**, **do**, **will**, etc.). An affirmative statement requires a negative tag question. A negative statement requires an affirmative tag question. The verb tense in the tag question should be the same as the verb tense in the main statement.

It is difficult, isn't it?   You like that, don't you?
+   –   +   –

It wasn't difficult, was it?   You don't like that, do you?
–   +   –   +

Tag Questions in the Present Tense with "Be"

Positive (+) to Negative (–)   **Negative (–) to Positive (+)**

| I am wrong, aren't I?* | I'm not wrong, am I? |

You are wrong, aren't you?   You aren't wrong, are you?

He is wrong, isn't he?	He isn't wrong, is he?
She is wrong, isn't she?	She isn't wrong, is she?
It is wrong, isn't it?	It isn't wrong, is it?

We are wrong, aren't we?   We aren't wrong, are we?
You are wrong, aren't you?   You aren't wrong, are you?
They are wrong, aren't they?   They aren't wrong, are they?

* Positive to negative tag questions with **I am** use the form **aren't I**.

A. Match the statement with the tag question,

1. John was really talented,   a) wasn't she?
2. Sue Mills is an athlete,   b) aren't I?
3. You aren't going to the game,   c) were we?
4. That book is a best-seller,   d) isn't she?
5. The skis we got were very expensive, e) weren't you?
6. I'm accepted into the program,   f) wasn't he?
7. He wasn't the famous gymnast,   g) was he?
8. She was a well-known skater,   h) are you?
9. You were at the show last night,   i) isn't it?
10. We weren't too early for dinner,   j) weren't they

cross-country
 skiing
downhill skiing
sailing
skate boarding
a hurdler

6   7   8   9   10

44

B. Write tag questions for these statements.

They were late, **weren't they**?

1. The water-skiing we did yesterday was fun,
2. The speakers weren't very well prepared,
3. Our Spanish teacher is absent today,
4. You are confused about the explanations,
5. Unemployment rates are down this year,
6. We aren't welcome at that party,
7. The photographer didn't forget his telephoto lens,
8. The bicycle wheel isn't loose,
9. I am too aggressive on the tennis court,
10. He isn't really qualified for this,

If the main statement has no auxiliary verb, use the dummy auxiliary **do, does** (present), or **did** (past).

You like parties, don't you?
 +   −

You don't like parties, do you?
 −   +

C. Match the statement and the tag question.

1. You don't really like this music,   a) does she?
2. They don't know what floor our office is on, b) didn't she?
3. She didn't apply for the job in time,   c) don't they?
4. He cleans the lens of his camera regularly,   d) do you?
5. You live near my aunt and uncle,   e) did she?
6. Sara went ice-fishing last winter,   f) do I?
7. I don't have to repeat this again,   g) doesn't he?
8. They still like to plant flowers in their garden, h) do they?
9. She doesn't have enough money for the opera, i) don't I?
10. I play backgammon quite often,   j) don't you?

electronic games bowling ping-pong a kite a frisbee		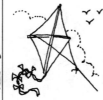			
	11	12	13	14	15

D. Write the tag questions for these statements.

1. Liz absolutely loves doing jigsaw puzzles,
2. Max didn't forget to lock the door,
3. You all enjoy playing the odd game of ping-pong,
4. Children generally like to play electronic games,
5. Those kids went bowling yesterday,
6. Skiers really don't mind cold weather,
7. A camera usually has a flash,
8. Francis Drake sailed around the world first,
9. We ate later than usual yesterday evening,
10. Jeff didn't play checkers yesterday,

UNDERSTAND: **Some Special Ways of Forming Tag Questions**

Indefinite Pronoun as Subject

If the subject in the main clause is **something, nothing,** or **everything,** ask the tag question with **it** as the subject.

Something is wrong, isn't it?

Nothing happened, did it?

TEACHER'S BOX: Indefinite pronouns carry either an affirmative or negative sense, so the choice of pronoun determines whether the tag is positive or negative: "Something was wrong, wasn't it?" "Nothing was wrong, was it?"

"There" as the Subject

If the subject in the main clause is **there,** ask the tag question with **there** as the subject.

There isn't any problem here, is there?

A. Write the tag questions for these statements. Use informal speech.

1. Everything is going well in the class,
2. There wasn't a very big crowd at the game last night,
3. Nothing interesting happened while I was away,
4. Everyone got a copy of yesterday's newspaper,

horseback riding gardening bird-watching curling photography					
	16	17	18	19	20

5. There didn't seem to be much interest in going scuba-diving,
6. There was a lot of excitement over the game,
7. No one had very much to say to the commission,
8. Everyone has handed in their assignments late,
9. Everyone seemed to be angry about the decision,
10. Nothing happened at the meeting yesterday,

Language in Transition

When the subject of a sentence is an indefinite pronoun (**everyone**, **someone**, **no one**, etc.), it is correct to use the singular pronoun (**he/she**) as the subject in the tag question. However, in contemporary English it is more common to use the plural pronoun (they), except in very formal usage.

UNDERSTAND: **Tag Questions with Two Auxiliary Verbs**

If there are two auxiliary verbs in a statement, use the first auxiliary to form the tag question.

He hasn't been working too hard, has he?
They should have been back by now, shouldn't they?

A. Write the tag questions for these statements.

1. The people who saw the accident have been having nightmares,
2. The government should have acted much sooner in this case,
3. We can't all win the lottery,
4. They wouldn't have gone there if they had known of the danger,
5. Nobody can really tell when another person is lying,
6. Winning the lottery has never brought happiness to anyone,
7. They haven't been working in the garden since this morning,
8. It won't be raining when we leave tomorrow evening,
9. We probably shouldn't believe everything the sales representative says,
10. We will never be able to forget her many dynamic speeches,

wheels a pedal spokes brakes handlebars			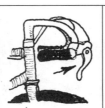		
	21	22	23	24	25

UNDERSTAND: **"I do too" and "So do I" to Agree with Affirmative Statements**

Use **too** to show agreement in short affirmative statements. Use **too** after a short affirmative statement. The word order for short statements with **too** is: subject + verb + **too**.

> I am tired.   **I am too**.   (present)
> He was happy.   **I was too**.   (past)

Use **too** after an object pronoun to express agreement informally.

> I am excited.   **Me too**.   (informal)

Use **so** to show agreement in short affirmative statements. Use **so** at the beginning of the short affirmative statement. The word order for short statements with **so** is: so + verb + subject.

> She is a good swimmer.   **So is he**.

Use the dummy auxiliary **do, does** (present), or **did** (past) if there is only a main verb in the original statement.

> I like chocolate.   **I do too**.
> She likes coffee.   **He does too**.
> He went to a movie last night.   **I did too**.

A. Write short statements of agreement using the auxiliary verb **do** in the correct form with **too**.

Karl enjoys photography. (Joe)   Joe does too.

1. Suzanne got excited about our trip to Paris. (I)
2. Richard works very hard at his job. (His colleague)
3. Anita's family lives in the suburbs. (Mine)
4. Alice met a lot of people from other countries. (We)
5. The Swiss girl lived with a American family in Florida. (Maria)
6. I really enjoyed my bicycle trip last summer. (John)
7. I made an appointment to see the ophthalmologist. (My friend)
8. Pamela and I studied Mandarin last term. (Dan and Geoff)
9. Bin sometimes has difficulty with her pronunciation. (Karl)
10. Gisela passed the TOEFL the first time she took it. (Her friend)

a lens a shutter film a counter a flash					
	26	27	28	29	30

48

B. Write short statements of agreement using **so** and the correct form of the auxiliary **do**.

They walked to class. (we)   So did we.

1. We play cards almost every day. (the Nakamuras)
2. They learned to ski when they were very young. (we)
3. I lived in an apartment by myself in Rome. (she)
4. My uncle likes to go mountain-climbing. (my father)
5. Mike practises basketball nearly every day. (his teammates)
6. She surfed every day when she was on holiday. (Sam)
7. My friend went bird-watching on her holiday. (Anna)
8. They meet in a restaurant for dinner once a month. (my friends and I)
9. Their university has strict attendance requirements. (ours)
10. The guests really enjoyed the party last night. (I)

UNDERSTAND: **"I don't either" and "Neither do I" to Agree with Negative Statements**

Use **either** to show agreement in short negative statements. Put **either** at the end of the short negative statement. The word order for short statements with **either** is: subject + verb + **either**.

| She isn't a good swimmer. | **He isn't either.** | (present) |
| They weren't very tired. | **We weren't either.** | (past) |

Use **neither** to show agreement in short negative statements. Put **neither** at the beginning of a short negative statement. The word order for short statements with **neither** is: **neither** + verb + subject.

| She is not tired. | **Neither am I.** | (present) |
| He wasn't happy. | **Neither was I.** | (past) |

> **TEACHER'S BOX:** An informal way to express agreement with a negative statement is to use the object pronoun + **neither**: "I don't like hot dogs. Me neither."

Use the same auxiliary as the original statement in short statements of agreement. If there are two auxiliaries, use the first auxiliary in the short statement of agreement.

He doesn't like gardening.	I don't either.
She can't drink coffee.	He can't either.
We haven't been living here long.	I haven't either.

| a jigsaw puzzle
chess
checkers
cards
backgammon |  |  |  |  | 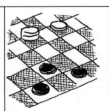 |
| | 31 | 32 | 33 | 34 | 35 |

A. Change the responses to the negative using auxiliary verb + **not** + **either**.

I don't like living here.

Neither does Susan.   **Susan doesn't either.**

1. Franco won't use a dictionary.
   Neither will I. _____

2. None of her classmates failed the test.
   Neither did mine. _____

3. They can't sing well.
   Neither can we. _____

4. Nadine never listens to rock music.
   Neither does Lynda. _____

5. The taxi driver didn't hear the address.
   Neither did I. _____

6. None of your friends went to the opera.
   Neither did mine. _____

7. Andrea didn't play the lottery.
   Neither did Tara. _____

8. Her bus wasn't on time yesterday.
   Neither was mine. _____

9. Miguel doesn't have any film.
   Neither does Jun. _____

10. I haven't had a holiday this year.
    Neither has Keiko. _____

B. Complete the sentences with **either** or **neither**.

1. Robert wasn't in class. _____ was Sally.

2. Keiko wasn't on time. Margot wasn't _____.

3. Margarita can't swim very well. _____ can Tom.

4. Poling hadn't gone wind-surfing before. _____ had Akiko.

5. Your friends don't go horseback riding. Mine don't _____.

6. The teacher wasn't born here. I wasn't _____.

7. Daniela didn't like the movie. Bob and Mary didn't _____.

8. Her brother isn't very tall. _____ is mine.

9. Carla's husband doesn't play tennis. Mine doesn't _____.

10. Rocco isn't good at snooker. _____ is Pedro.

classical music rock music opera snooker playing the lottery					
	36	37	38	39	40

C.   Find the errors and correct them. Check (✔) sentences that are correct.

1.   I don't like living alone. Susan doesn't neither.
2.   Franco won't use a dictionary. Either will I.
3.   None of the students failed the test. Either did I.
4.   They can't play classical music. We can't either.
5.   Nadine never smokes cigarettes. I don't either.
6.   The taxi driver didn't hear the address. Either did I.
7.   None of my friends saw the scary movie on TV last night. I didn't either.
8.   Tara didn't take her frisbee. Andrea didn't neither.
9.   Your bus wasn't on time yesterday. Neither was mine.
10.   Miguel doesn't play chess. I don't neither.

Vocabulary Challenge

Leisure Activities

Each box contains four words. Three of the words are similar. The word that is different should be "bumped out" to the next box. The next box will also contain three similar words, and one word that does not fit.

Students should continue bumping the words until they reach the end. Then they must use the remaining word to complete the sentence at the bottom. The first box is done as an example.

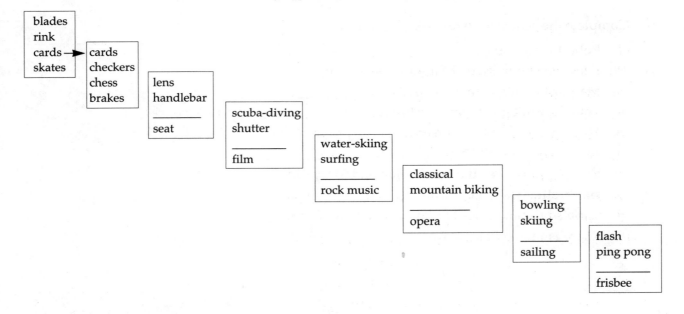

You will remember these words in a _____ if you study the picture dictionary, won't you?

Ten-Minute Grammar Games

Stump the Expert

Focus: Practise using tag questions.

Each student thinks of a subject that he or she knows a lot about (hobbies, sports, special interests, etc.), and writes it on a piece of paper, next to his or her name. The teacher collects the pieces of paper, and lists the subjects on the board.

Students work in teams to write questions to stump the experts, using tag questions.

The teacher chooses an "expert" to begin, and other students take turns asking their questions. The first person to stump the expert wins, and takes over as the expert.

Small Talk

Focus: Practise using tag questions.

Students work with the following scenario: They are at a party, and have just been introduced to someone they find interesting and would like to get to know better. They are trying to make small talk to keep the conversation going.

Students work in pairs to write a dialogue. They use as many tag questions as they can, trying to illicit agreement from their partners.

Students can then read their conversations to the class. Warning: These can be quite funny!

Test Yourself

A. Write tag questions to complete these sentences.

1. That girl is too shy to be in a variety show,
2. He comes from somewhere in northeastern Poland,
3. You haven't got much time before your performance,
4. Everything is going to be ready for the performance,
5. The star of the show wouldn't refuse to perform,
6. People couldn't swim in that river because of pollution,
7. Almost everyone thought that it was a wonderful idea,
8. Lea had to resign from her job at the Ministry of Finance,
9. George isn't a very honest tax accountant,
10. The trip we made to New Zealand was very expensive,
11. Hard work generally brings its own rewards,
12. Something strange is going on around here,
13. We will be able to go to the beach later today,
14. Something went wrong with their plans to buy a car,
15. You don't remember who made that brilliant suggestion,

52

B. Complete the short dialogues with **too** or **so**.

   1. Janet is really good at basketball.
Oh really? My sister is _____.

   2. I'm going to that dinner party next week.
What a surprise! I am _____.

   3. We had the most incredible trip last summer.
_____ did we.

   4. Jason has bought an old bike with broken spokes.
What a coincidence! _____ has my brother.

   5. My aunt and uncle have twin daughters.
I don't believe it! Mine do _____.

   6. My father was stuck in that traffic jam yesterday.
_____ was I. It was terrible.

   7. Our teacher is really pleased with our grades.
Ours is _____.

   8. The bus to Toronto is always on time.
_____ is the bus to San Francisco.

   9. We have decided to go on a picnic next weekend.
_____ have we. Maybe we could go together.

  10. Canada is officially a bilingual country. What about your country?
My country is _____.

C. Agree with the following statements. Use short statements with **so** or **neither** + the appropriate auxiliary verb.

I can't wait for the party. **Neither can I.**

   1. I enjoy being alone sometimes.
   2. I have never been wind-surfing.
   3. I have been practising my English a lot recently.
   4. I always forget people's names after we meet.
   5. I didn't get to the concert on time.
   6. I won't watch curling on TV tomorrow.
   7. I should get more exercise during the winter.
   8. I thought about changing my philosophy course last semester.
   9. I would like to be fluent in at least two languages.
  10. I'm going to start my computer course next month.
  11. I can water-ski really well after those lessons.
  12. I didn't really enjoy that meal very much.
  13. I don't like playing tennis when the weather is too hot.
  14. I usually shop for groceries on the weekend.
  15. I learned to cook from my paternal grandmother.

Score for Test Yourself: _____

Vocabulary Answers

1. scuba-diving
2. windsurfing
3. water-skiing
4. mountain-biking
5. surfing
6. sailing
7. downhill skiing
8. a hurdler
9. cross-country skiing
10. skate boarding
11. ping-pong
12. a kite
13. electronic games
14. a frisbee
15. bowling
16. photography
17. horseback riding
18. curling
19. bird-watching
20. gardening
21. spokes
22. wheels
23. brakes
24. handlebars
25. a pedal
26. a counter
27. a flash
28. a lens
29. film
30. a shutter
31. chess
32. backgammon
33. cards
34. a jigsaw puzzle
35. checkers
36. snooker
37. opera
38. playing the lottery
39. classical music
40. rock music

5 Review Unit

TOEFL® Test Practice Exercises

You have 25 minutes to complete these exercises. When you complete Part A, continue to Part B. An answer sheet is provided on page 193.

Part A

Choose the phrase that best completes the sentence. Blacken the letter that corresponds to your answer on the answer sheet.

Example: Since moving to live near the airport, the Smiths _____ a great deal of noise.
     (a) learned to lives with
     (b) have learned to live with
     (c) have learned living with
     (d) learning to live with

       (A) (B) (C) (D)

1. What happened after the environmental protection laws were passed _____ unique.
     (a) wasn't neither surprising nor
     (b) was neither surprising or
     (c) wasn't either surprising nor
     (d) was neither surprising nor

2. _____ new workers once they were sure that the recession was really over.
     (a) The company start to hire
     (b) The company starts hiring
     (c) The company starts to hire
     (d) The company started hiring

3. _____ by embracing teachings that promise to redeem their honour?
   (a) What these young men and women have to losing
   (b) What do these young men and women have lose
   (c) What do these young men and women have to lose
   (d) What do have these young men and women to lose

4. Since viewing his first total eclipse in Manitoba in 1979, _____ from Kenya to Indonesia to Mexico.
   (a) he has taken him
   (b) the quest has taken him
   (c) he has taken his quest
   (d) it has taken him

5. The debate over whether someone with an artistic temperament can relate to someone with a scientific mind _____.
   (a) has been going on for centuries
   (b) have been going on for centuries
   (c) were going on for centuries
   (d) has being going on for centuries

6. The judge says that the company _____ by terminating it abruptly, but has also ignored two court orders.
   (a) have not only broken the contract
   (b) had not only broken the contract
   (c) has not only broken the contract
   (d) was not only broken the contract

7. Adherents believed _____ the world as we know it would come to an end and the spirits of their ancestors would be resurrected.
   (a) if they keeps dancing
   (b) that they keep dancing
   (c) that if they kept dancing
   (d) if they are keep dancing

8. The rescue workers _____ all night, but the street is still full of debris after the earthquake.
   (a) are working
   (b) have been working
   (c) have been worked
   (d) work

9. That interesting man we were talking to has been a musician all his life, _____?
   (a) did he not
   (b) isn't he
   (c) hasn't he
   (d) wasn't he

10. The professor was not satisfied with the way the class went yesterday, and _____ most of the students.

    (a) either were
    (b) neither weren't
    (c) either wasn't
    (d) neither were

11. A survey revealed today that, although in some places the number of smokers _____, in others it has been increasing.

    (a) decreasing
    (b) has decreased
    (c) is decreased
    (d) was decreased

12. The teenager's parents made him _____ not to come home after ten o'clock on school nights.

    (a) to promise
    (b) promise
    (c) will promise
    (d) promised

13. A lot of people prefer _____ in large crowded cities to having a residence in the countryside.

    (a) living
    (b) lived
    (c) to have lived
    (d) to have been living

14. The spectators at the championship hockey game breathed a sigh of relief when the star player _____.

    (a) has returned to the ice
    (b) was returned to the ice
    (c) did return to the ice
    (d) returned to the ice

15. The first violent incident _____ during the political campaign that took place five years ago.

    (a) was occurred
    (b) have been occurred
    (c) occurring
    (d) occurred

58

Part B

One of the underlined grammar points in each sentence is incorrect. Blacken the the letter that corresponds to the error on the answer sheet.

Example: A group of Canadian researchers <u>have reported</u>^A yesterday <u>that</u>^B they have <u>found</u>^C evidence that genetic mutations <u>cause</u>^D incurable Alzheimer's disease.

(A) (B) (C) (D)

16. So far, <u>the companies</u>^A short history <u>has included</u>^B convictions <u>for</u>^C environmental offences <u>in several</u>^D different countries.

17. Several reports <u>have been publish</u>^A over the last decade but <u>there</u>^B has been <u>no</u>^C reaction <u>from</u>^D the government.

18. A survey <u>sponsored by</u>^A the student association <u>found</u>^B that students <u>don't drink</u>^C often but that when they do, they frequently <u>overconsumes</u>^D.

19. A poll found <u>that</u>^A the number of students on campus <u>which</u>^B drink <u>has remained</u>^C steady but that the number of students who drink excessively <u>has gone up</u>^D.

20. Although people <u>has reported</u>^A problems with pre-authorized automatic debits from <u>their</u>^B bank accounts, plans <u>to remove</u>^C safeguards will go <u>ahead</u>^D.

21. In Thailand, <u>the best</u>^A places for <u>view</u>^B the total eclipse <u>will be</u>^C in <u>the</u>^D northwestern and northeastern provinces.

22. He <u>called</u>^A the book a science-fiction version of <u>that</u>^B he <u>himself</u>^C <u>had been doing</u>^D for the past twenty-five years.

23. The speaker <u>received</u>^A hearty applause from the audience <u>when</u>^B she talked about <u>give</u>^C back her medal as a protest against nuclear <u>testing</u>^D.

24. She couldn't help <u>return</u>^A to the theatre <u>to look</u>^B once more at the stage <u>where</u>^C she had launched her illustrious <u>acting</u>^D career.

25. The need <u>for</u>^A stop talking and take action <u>becomes</u>^B apparent as you view the destruction that <u>has been caused</u>^C around here <u>over</u>^D the years.

26. <u>Just before</u>^A the end of the nineteenth century, <u>a</u>^B Paiute medicine man began <u>preach</u>^C the benefits of <u>the</u>^D Ghost Dance.

27. People in Alaska <u>have learned</u>^A to <u>living</u>^B with extremes of weather, and <u>there are</u>^C outdoor activities <u>even</u>^D in the dark days of winter.

28. On the city's hiking trails, you can take a walk or a bike ride in the wilderness without
    A   B   C
    leave the city.
    D

29. The heroine of the play is very determined and no one can stopping her from getting
                              A   B   C
    the man she wants.
                    D

30. The three armies that have been fought for more than three years took a step towards
                      A   B
    peace as negotiations began last week.
          C   D

31. Bread-baking is surging in popularity these days, and also is the interest in all kinds of
                  A   B   C   D
    bread-making machines.

32. A square will officially be named in honour of the woman who put so much personal
                            A   B   C
    effort and money into help the poor.
                          D

33. Poachers, who traditionally hunted rhinos to sell their horns as an aphrodisiac
              A   B
    has turned their attention towards tame animals in zoos and safari parks.
    C   D

34. The group of friends didn't left the party until they had helped to clean up all the mess
                      A   B   C
    the guests had made.
                D

35. Experts have known for a long time that get no exercise was bad for us, but now they
                                            A   B
    are saying too much exercise is also dangerous for your health.
              C   D

36. While other species of bear hibernate in winter, polar bears remain active, for travel
          A   B   C
    across the sea ice to hunt for food.
                      D

37. The reason that the children look so completely exhausted is that they have
               A   B
    being running around playing outside all day.
    C   D

38. Some sociologists believe that regulate television violence is difficult because it doesn't
    A   B   C
    offend everyone equally.
           D

39. Many scientists believe the untimely arrival of a mammoth meteorite kill off the
         A   B   C
    dinosaurs approximately 65 million years ago.
                                            D

40. Entomologists have discovered that the first land animals similar to today's centipedes
                  A   B
    and millipedes first have eaten dirt and then consumed each other.
                        C   D

| 6 | Past Perfect Aspect
Past Perfect with "Before," "After," and "When"
Past Perfect with "By the time"
Using "Hope" and "Wish" |
|---|---|

What Do You Know?

A Year in Your Life

Choose a year of your life to relive. List five things that you wish you had done that year. List five things that you wish you hadn't done that year.

Discuss your list with a partner.

Understanding Grammar

UNDERSTAND: **Past Perfect Aspect**

The perfective aspect is used to express the relationship between two times. The past perfect relates two past times to describe two actions in the past, one of which occurred before the other.

The past perfect is used to describe the action that happened earlier in the past, and the simple past is used to describe the action that happened in the more recent past.

The robber **had run** away when the police **arrived**.
        Past perfect   Simple past

Both actions are in past time but one occurred before the other. First, the robber ran away. Second, the police arrived. Compare this with a sentence that describes two actions that happened at the same time in the past:

The robber **ran** away when the police **arrived**.
      Simple past   Simple past

To form the past perfect, use the past tense of the auxiliary verb **have** (which indicates perfective aspect). Use the past participle of the main verb.

I had eaten…

Affirmative		Contraction	
I had		I'd	
you had		you'd	
he had		he'd	
she had		she'd	
it had	eaten	it'd	eaten
we had		we'd	
you had		you'd	
they had		they'd	

A. Complete the sentences using the past perfect form of the verb.

1. When Jack reached into his pocket, he realized that he_____(lose) wallet.

2. The pilot was not nervous on the flight because he _____ (fly) before.

3. Robert didn't want to go to the exhibition with us because he _____(go) the day before.

4. My uncle offered to drive the big bus because he _____(drive) one before.

a hose a fire hydrant a fire extinguisher a ladder an axe					
	1	2	3	4	5

5. The athlete _____ (win) many national competitions before he started competing internationally.

6. The accountant _____ (work) for the same company for half a century when he retired last month.

7. By the time the politician realized that his party was in trouble, he _____ (lose) most of his supporters.

8. The students couldn't go on holiday until they _____ (hand in) all their overdue assignments.

9. The robbers _____ (escape) with all the money by the time the police arrived at the bank.

10. By the end of the wedding banquet, everyone _____ (eat) far too much.

The past perfect is often used to talk about a past action that had already occurred when a second, past action took place. **Already** is used in affirmative sentences. Put **already** between the auxiliary verb and the main verb.

When we arrived at the station, the train had **already** left.

B. Choose the best verb to complete the sentences. Put the verb in the past perfect with **already**.

stop   turn down   be   play   put out   start   have   go   leave   be married

1. When we got to the concert, the violinist _____ the first piece.

2. My grandparents _____ three children when my mother was born.

3. My cousin _____ the leak when the plumber arrived at the house.

4. When we got to the party last night, most of the other guests _____ home.

5. When the firefighters got there, the neighbours _____ the fire with a hose.

6. The customer _____ the store when the clerk noticed the mistake in the bill.

7. We _____ eating dinner when Tom and Jack finally got home from football practice.

8. Paula and Ricardo _____ for five or six years when we first met them.

9. When the alarm clock rang, Joseph _____ awake for nearly an hour.

10. When we phoned to complain about the noise, the people next door _____ the loud music.

a fire engine a firefighter rubber boots an oxygen mask a safety net					
	6	7	8	9	10

UNDERSTAND: **Past Perfect with Expressions of Time**

Certain time expressions are commonly used with the past perfect. They are used to signal the order of two events that both occurred in past time.

after	After we had eaten dinner, we ordered coffee. (First, we ate dinner. Second, we ordered coffee.)
before	Before we ate dinner, we had felt hungry. (First, we felt hungry. Second, we ate dinner.)
when	When we arrived, our friends had already ordered. (First, our friends ordered. Then we arrived.)

A. Choose the best word to complete the sentence.

1. He had worked for the company for ten years (when / after) he was dismissed.
2. They had known each other for two years (before / after) they decided to get married.
3. (After / Before) she had exercised in the gym for one hour, she began to feel relaxed.
4. I had finished dinner (when / after) the telephone began to ring.
5. We had not got back to the hotel (after / when) we heard the news.
6. She had graduated from university (before / after) she thought of getting married.
7. My friend had lived in several different countries (after / when) he decided to settle in Canada.
8. They had been married for five years (when / after) they decided to have a child.
9. (After / when) he had made many great movies, the actor died in a tragic accident.
10. Our neighbours had lived in the same apartment for many years (when / after) they bought a house.

an accident skid marks a flat tire a tow truck a winch			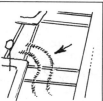		
	11	12	13	14	15

UNDERSTAND: **Past Perfect with "By the time"**

Use the expression **by the time** to relate two events in the past. Use **by the time** with the past tense. Use the past perfect in the main clause.

By the time means at the moment a past action took place or before that point in time.

> Everyone had left **by the time** we arrived. (Everyone left. Then we arrived.)

A. Combine the following pairs of sentences using "by the time."

> We got to the bus terminal. The bus left.
>
> **By the time we got to the terminal, the bus had left.**

1. She lost the election. She had been prime minister for ten years.
2. He learned to speak English. He had been in Australia for one year.
3. The painter was 80 years old. He had painted hundreds of paintings.
4. The hitchhiker got to his destination. He had been on the road for three days.
5. We finished the project in Thailand. We had worked on it for a year.
6. They had all finished writing the difficult math exam. The bell rang.
7. The paramedics had finished their work. The ambulance arrived.
8. They had played 36 holes of golf. It started to rain.
9. My appetizer came to the table late. Everyone else had finished theirs.
10. She had waited in the rain for 15 minutes. The bus finally arrived.

UNDERSTAND: **Past Perfect Aspect Negative Form**

Use the negative form of the past perfect to describe something that had not happened when another past action occurred.

> We hadn't been there five minutes when it began to rain.

Put **not** or **never** after the auxiliary verb **had** to form the past perfect negative.

Negative		**Contraction**	
I had not		I hadn't	
you had not		you hadn't	
he had not		he hadn't	
she had not		she hadn't	
it had not	eaten	it hadn't	eaten
we had not		we hadn't	
you had not		you hadn't	
they had not		they hadn't	

an ambulance paramedics a stretcher a sling crutches					
	16	**17**	**18**	**19**	**20**

A. Complete the sentences using the negative form of the past perfect.

Suzanne **had not studied** (not/study) English long when she arrived in this country.

1. Max was very nervous when he first arrived in Vancouver because he _____ (not/be) away from home before.
2. Alex was very excited about trying sushi in a Japanese restaurant because he _____ (never/taste) raw fish before.
3. The police officer _____ (not finish) her long distance conversation when the other line rang.
4. We _____ (not/live) in our new apartment for long when a robber broke in.
5. When the fire alarm went off in the hotel, the guests _____ (not/unpack) their suitcases.
6. The sales representative _____ (not/work) for the company for even a year when she got a promotion.
7. The famous couple _____ (not/tell) anyone about their wedding plans when they read about themselves in the paper.
8. We _____ (not/finish) our dessert when the waiter told us the restaurant was closing.
9. Karine _____ (never/see) a live concert when she bought tickets to see the Rolling Stones.
10. Bob and Maggie _____ (not/know) each other very long when they decided to get married.

UNDERSTAND: **Past Perfect Aspect Question Form**

Use the past perfect to ask questions about actions that took place before past actions that you already know about.

Had the movie started by the time you got your ticket?

To form a question with the past perfect, put the auxiliary verb **had** before the subject.

She arrived at eight. Had you eaten already?

had I
had you
had he
had she
had it   eaten?
had we
had you
had they

a police officer a robber a gun a mask a thief				
21	22	23	24	25

A. Match the statements and questions.

John went to bed late. Had he finished his homework?

1. There was an impressive thunderstorm last night.
2. Lili and Mike got married last weekend.
3. The flood waters broke through the dyke at 3 a.m.
4. The man in the patrol car was wearing handcuffs.
5. Indurian won the Tour de France in 1995.
6. I really enjoyed the piano recital last night.
7. Gabrielle really seemed to know her way around.
8. Peter was smiling when I got to his birthday party.
9. The students were really shocked when they failed the course.
10. Phil had an accident on the construction site.

a) Had he already opened his present?
b) Had you heard that pianist play before?
c) Had she been to Indonesia before?
d) Had people moved to higher ground?
e) Had he ever won it before?
f) Had the meteorology department issued a warning?
g) Had he been warned that it was dangerous there?
h) Had they known each other very long?
i) Had anyone failed the course before?
j) Had he committed a crime?

UNDERSTAND: **"Hope" and "Wish"**

Both **hope** and **wish** are used to describe situations you would like to happen in future. **Hope** describes future possibilities. **Wish** describes hypothetical (unreal) situations.

Hope

Hope describes things that are possible. You don't know, however, whether they will happen or not.

I hope it won't rain tomorrow.
I hope you like the present.

a patrol car handcuffs a badge a pickpocket a hold-up					
	26	**27**	**28**	**29**	**30**

A. Match the situations with the responses below.

1. Jane's house is a mess.
2. Mr. Tan's lawn is getting very dry.
3. That building is on fire.
4. Fraser looks pretty sad.
5. The Johnsons are coming to dinner.
6. Some people seem to be injured.
7. A pipe in my basement is leaking.
8. Alex has been working on his degree for years.
9. Jack is supposed to play football this afternoon.
10. The Kiers have applied for a bank loan.

a) I hope they will arrive on time.
b) He hopes to graduate this July.
c) He hopes it will rain soon.
d) She hopes no one drops over.
e) I hope someone called an ambulance.
f) I hope nothing bad has happened.
g) He hopes it won't rain during the game.
h) They hope to have news from the bank soon.
i) I hope the fire department comes quickly.
j) Let's hope the plumber gets here soon.

To react to statements by saying what you would like to happen or not happen in future, use the short answer forms, **I hope so, I hope not**.

Will the bus arrive on time?
I don't know. I hope so.

Will it rain tomorrow?
I don't know. I hope not.

B. Match the questions with the pictures on page 69.

1. Is he going to drop anything?
2. Are they going to miss the train?
3. Will the dinner be good?
4. Will they be late for work?
5. Did she pass her exam?
6. Is she going to give us a lot of homework?
7. Do you think it will rain?
8. Will the plumber be here soon?
9. Will he escape?

a leak a plumber to drip a plunger a pipe wrench					
	31	32	33	34	35

C. Give responses to the questions above with, **I hope so** or **I hope not**.

Wish

Wish describes unreal situations. Use **I wish** to express things you would hypothetically like to do (even though they are unreal possibilities). **I wish** is followed by a noun clause (either with or without **that**).

> I wish (that) I had time for a movie. (I don't.)
>
> I wish (that) I could fly. (I can't.)

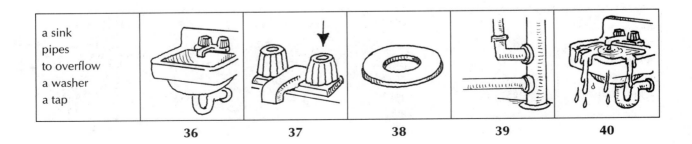

a sink pipes to overflow a washer a tap					
	36	**37**	**38**	**39**	**40**

70

The verb in the clause after **wish** is expressed in an earlier time than the situation that led to the wish.

Present:	I don't have much energy.
Past:	I wish I **had** more (energy).
Present:	He can't come for the meeting.
Past:	I wish he **could** (come).
Past:	I got to work late this morning.
Past perfect:	I wish I **had** left the house earlier.
Present perfect:	I haven't seen that movie.
Past perfect:	I wish I **had** (seen it).

A. Complete the sentence with the correct form of the verb.

It gets dark early in winter.
I wish it didn't.

It got dark early in winter.
I wish it hadn't.

1. We don't have enough time to finish.
   I wish we _____.

2. They can't speak English well.
   I wish they _____.

3. It hasn't rained for a month.
   The farmers wish it _____.

4. We didn't have anything to eat at noon today.
   We wish we _____.

5. I don't go to meetings often.
   I wish I _____.

6. They fell asleep during the speech.
   They wish they _____.

7. I stayed up very late last night.
   I wish I _____.

8. You don't agree with me.
   I wish you _____.

9. I can't remember how to get there.
   I wish I _____.

10. I didn't wear my rubber boots.
    I wish I _____.

Language in Transition

When the verb in the situation described is **be**, the verb in the noun clause is **were** for all persons and numbers: "Janet is mean. I wish she **weren't** so mean."

However, it is acceptable in informal contexts to ignore this rule: 'Janet is mean. I wish she **wasn't** so mean."

---

an earthquake a flood a tornado a blizzard a hurricane					
	41	42	43	44	45

> **TEACHER'S BOX:** **Wish** has a different meaning when it is used in some common special expressions such as **wish someone a happy birthday**, **wish someone good luck**, **wish someone a safe trip**: "John wrote to wish her a happy birthday." "I wish you good luck with your future studies." "They wished us a safe trip."

Vocabulary Challenge

Emergencies

Put these words into categories. You should have five groups of five words each.

> earthquake   paramedics   leak   flood   fire hydrant   stretcher   plumber   tow truck   plunger   axe   hose   skid-marks   tornado   accident   pipe wrench   ambulance   winch   blizzard   crutches   flat tire   overflow   fire extinguisher   ladder   sling   hurricane

Ten-Minute Grammar Games

Hopes and Wishes

Focus: Practise using **hope** and **wish**.

The teacher writes the name of each student on a piece of paper, folds it over, and puts it in a bag. Each student selects a piece of paper, and writes a hope or wish for the person chosen. The hopes or wishes should follow these criteria:

a) They should always be positive, not negative.

b) They should be based, as much as possible, on a distinctive (positive!) characteristic of the other student.

> I hope he gets the job he wants.
>
> I wish she could visit her cousins in Spain next summer.

Students take turns reading their hopes and wishes for their classmates aloud, **without** mentioning the name of the person they have chosen. Other students try to guess who the person is.

Three Wishes

Focus: Practise using **hope** and **wish**.

Students imagine that they have each been granted three wishes. They should think about the wishes they would choose, and then write them down.

In groups, students discuss their three wishes.

Note: Wishes should not be used to grant additional wishes!

Test Yourself

A. Write the past perfect form of the following verbs.

fly   had flown

1.	go	11.	eat
2.	knew	12.	understand
3.	become	13.	throw
4.	wear	14.	drive
5.	take	15.	speak
6.	have	16.	steal
7.	find	17.	wake
8.	drink	18.	begin
9.	give	19.	break
10.	be	20.	blow

B. Put the verbs in brackets in the correct tense

After they (live) in Mexico one year, they (speak) Spanish well.

After they **had lived** in Mexico one year, they **spoke** Spanish well.

1. When the guests _____ (go) home, the hosts _____ (clean up) the recreation room.
2. After they _____ (eat), they _____ (go) to the living room for coffee.
3. When the speaker _____ (finish) his speech, everyone _____ (applaud) vigorously.
4. Before the exam _____ (end), most of the students _____ (hand in) their papers.
5. After the meeting _____ (began), someone_____ (knock) at the door.
6. The team _____ (leave) the locker room quickly after the coach _____ (announce) the next day's schedule.
7. By the time we _____ (arrive), the other guests _____ (go) home already.
8. After they _____ (check) our passports, they _____ (give) us our boarding passes.
9. Before I _____ (go) swimming, I _____ (put on) my bathing cap.
10. The team _____ (put on) their uniforms by the time the game _____ (start).

C. Complete the sentences with **hope** or **wish**. Use the correct tense.

1. The ambassador _____ he could speak better French.
2. We _____ you will be comfortable during your stay.
3. Tara _____ she'll have good marks in her math test.
4. I _____ I had more money to spend on books.

5. The manager _____ you have enjoyed your stay.

6. We _____ we had met each other 20 years ago.

7. Hiroshi _____ he had taken more pictures in New York.

8. I _____ June hadn't called me so late last night.

9. I _____ I'm not calling you too late.

10. The athlete _____ she had won a medal at the Olympics.

Score for Test Yourself: _____
$$\overline{40}$$

Vocabulary Answers

1. a fire extinguisher	16. a stretcher	31. a plunger
2. a ladder	17. crutches	32. to drip
3. a hose	18. a sling	33. a pipe wrench
4. an axe	19. an ambulance	34. a leak
5. a fire hydrant	20. paramedics	35. a plumber
6. rubber boots	21. a mask	36. a sink
7. a fire engine	22. a thief	37. a tap
8. an oxygen mask	23. a gun	38. a washer
9. a safety net	24. a police officer	39. pipes
10. a firefighter	25. a robber	40. to overflow
11. a winch	26. a badge	41. a hurricane
12. a tow truck	27. a patrol car	42. a tornado
13. skid marks	28. handcuffs	43. a flood
14. a flat tire	29. a hold-up	44. an earthquake
15. an accident	30. a pickpocket	45. a blizzard

<table>
<tr><td>

7

</td><td>

Conditional Sentences
Conditional I, II, III
Conditional with "Unless"

</td></tr>
</table>

What Do You Know?

What Would You Do?

Look at the list of activities and list them in the categories on page 76.

1. go bungee jumping
2. cheat on an important exam
3. return extra change that you receive by mistake in a store
4. tell a friend her new haircut looks awful
5. ride in a hot-air balloon
6. lend money to an acquaintance
7. cram for an exam
8. not leave a tip for bad restaurant service
9. lie about past experience in a job interview
10. take a day off class to have fun

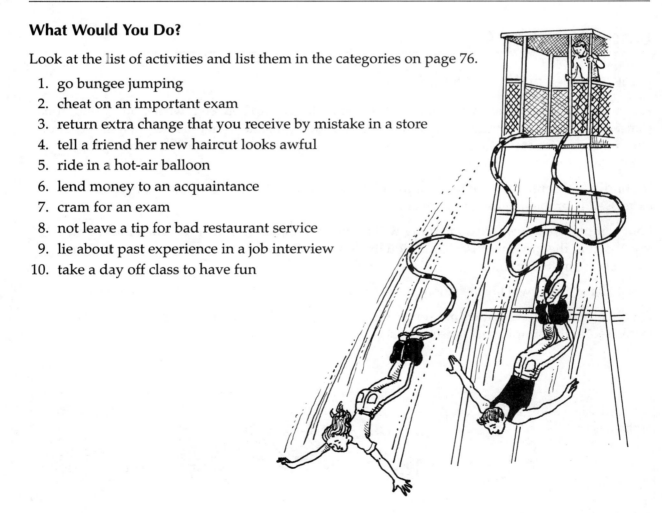

I would do this	I might do this	I would never do this

Understanding Grammar

UNDERSTAND: Conditional Sentences

A conditional sentence is used to show an **if**/**then** relationship between two actions. Conditional clauses generally contain **if** and they describe an action (or state) that must happen in order for another action (or state) to take place. We can call the **if** clause the **condition clause** and the main clause the **result clause**.

In conditional sentences, the tense of the verb in the **if** clause tells us whether the condition expressed is probably going to happen.

For example, we know that something will probably happen in the future when the **if** clause is expressed in the present tense. Conditional I expresses the **if** clause in present time and the main clause in future time.

    If I **have** time, I **will file** the reports. (I may have time later and I will probably file the reports.)

On the other hand, we know that something is very unlikely to happen when the **if** clause is expressed in the simple past tense.

a fax machine				
a photocopier				
a computer				
a typewriter				
a modem				
	1	**2**	**3**	**4**	**5**

Conditional II expresses the **if** clause in past time and the main clause with **would** + base form of the verb.

> If I **had** time, I **would file** the reports. (I don't have time and there is little chance I will file the reports.)

Similarly, we know that something did not happen when the **if** clause is expressed as a hypothetical situation in past time with the past perfect tense. Conditional III expresses the **if** clause in past time (past perfect) and the main clause with **would** and the present perfect form of the main verb.

> If I **had had** time, I **would have filed** the reports. (I didn't have time and I didn't file the reports.)

UNDERSTAND: **Conditional I**

Use Conditional I for real future possibility. The **if** clause gives the condition that will make a future action possible.

> If X happens, then Y will happen.
>   Condition   Result

Use the present tense in the **if** clause. Use the future form in the result (main) clause.

> If it **is** sunny, we **will go**.
>   Present   Future

The **if** clause can be first or last in the sentence with no change in meaning.

> If it is sunny, we will go.
> We will go if it is sunny.

A. Match the clauses to make logical sentences.

1. If there is a snowstorm tonight,
2. If you work more carefully,
3. If we buy a fax machine,
4. If we have enough players,
5. If I don't have to work late,
6. If we keep more regular hours,
7. If you want to have a coffee break,
8. If they insist on speaking their own language,
9. If the tickets are still available,
10. If you practise hard,

a) you will have a better chance of making the finals.
b) I will go to the health club with you.
c) we will feel more rested and relaxed.
d) they will not make good progress in English.
e) the office will run more smoothly.
f) we will join you at the concert hall.
g) I will cover for you at the reception desk.
h) we will be able to form a team.
i) you will make fewer mistakes.
j) the streets will be dangerous.

a keyboard a monitor a printer a diskette a mouse					
	6	7	8	9	10

Conditional I Negative Form

One or both clauses in a conditional sentence can be negative. The **if** clause is in present time and the main clause is in future time. The negative form of **will** is **won't** (**will not**).

> If it **rains**, we **won't go**.
> If it **doesn't rain**, we **will go**.
> If it **isn't** sunny, we **won't go**.

A. Choose the correct clause to complete these sentences logically.

1. If you get to the office late,
   a) you'll find a parking spot.
   b) you won't find a parking spot.

2. If you order your supplies early,
   a) you won't run out.
   b) you'll run out.

3. If you aren't careful,
   a) you won't get hurt.
   b) you'll get hurt.

4. If he smokes cigarettes,
   a) he'll stay healthy.
   b) he won't stay healthy.

5. If they don't clean up the stockroom,
   a) the manager will be pleased.
   b) the manager won't be pleased.

6. If they don't hurry up,
   a) they won't be on time.
   b) they'll be on time.

7. If he doesn't stop smoking,
   a) it will affect his health.
   b) it won't affect his health.

8. If I find the missing file,
   a) my boss will be happy.
   b) my boss won't be happy.

9. If the filing cabinet is full,
   a) we'll need a new one.
   b) we won't need a new one.

10. If they drive carelessly,
    a) they'll have an accident.
    b) they'll won't have an accident.

Conditional I Question Form

The **if** clause in a question is always expressed in present time. The main clause is expressed in future time. The **if** clause may appear either at the beginning or the end of the sentence.

> **Will** they **cancel** the order if the delivery **is** late?
> If we **are** late for the meeting, **will** they **let** us in?

a storeroom
a filing cabinet
book shelves
a bulletin board
a stockroom

 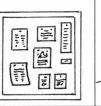 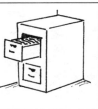 

11   12   13   14   15

A. Match the two parts of the sentence.

1. What on earth will we do
2. Will the new geography teacher be angry
3. If there is another big blizzard,
4. If I speak English with a strong accent,
5. How will we use the computer
6. Will they go swimming tomorrow morning
7. If this terrible summer drought continues,
8. If I exercise vigorously every day,
9. If the phone keeps ringing,
10. Where will we put the photocopier

a) if some students forget to bring their books?
b) will the man in the street understand me?
c) if there is a shark warning posted at the beach?
d) if the photocopier breaks down?
e) if it doesn't come with a mouse?
f) will they be able to clear the snow fast enough?
g) if there is no room at the reception area?
h) what will happen to the farmers' crops?
i) will the answering machine take the call?
j) will I really be in better shape and have more energy?

> **TEACHER'S BOX:** Conditional sentences that use the present tense in both clauses can be used to express factual conditions (universal truths): "If you try hard, you never lose." "If a glass of water is exposed to air, eventually it evaporates."

UNDERSTAND: **"Unless" in Conditional Sentences**

When the **if** clause expresses a negative condition, **unless** can be used to replace **if** + negative form of the auxiliary verb. There is no change in meaning.

> If you don't hurry, you'll be late.
> Unless you hurry, you'll be late.

stationery
letterhead
a document
supplies
a memo

16   17   18   19   20

80

A. Rewrite these sentences using **unless**.

If you don't study, you'll fail. **Unless you study, you'll fail.**

1. I can't take a holiday if I don't finish the project.
2. If you don't have a good knowledge of English, you can't apply for the job.
3. We can't return the merchandise if we don't have receipts.
4. The children won't get dessert if they don't finish their vegetables.
5. If the smokers don't put out their cigarettes, they can't enter the conference room.
6. The bank won't give people loans if they don't have jobs.
7. If I don't pass the TOEFL exam, I will not be able to get into university.
8. If people aren't wearing formal clothes, the restaurant won't let them in.
9. The planet will not survive if we don't take care of the environment.
10. The exam will not start if everyone is not present.

B. Use your own ideas to complete the sentences, using **unless** to give conditions.

They'll cut off your phone unless (you pay your bill).

1. We will deplete our energy resources unless _____.
2. Society will become more violent unless _____.
3. Unless _____, traffic in big cities will get worse.
4. It will become more difficult for young people to get jobs unless _____.
5. Unless _____, overpopulation will continue to increase.
6. People will become more alienated unless _____.
7. Unless _____, you cannot become really fluent in another language.
8. You will not enjoy travelling in other countries unless _____.
9. Unless _____, global warming will worsen.
10. Racism will continue to exist unless _____.

TEACHER'S BOX: Unless is often used to deliver threats concerning negative consequences: "Unless you clean your room, you won't get your allowance."

---

a clipboard a stapler correction fluid a business card a rotary file					
	21	22	23	24	25

UNDERSTAND: **Conditional II**

Use Conditional II (present unreal) for hypothetical or imaginary situations. Use the **if** clause to express the hypothetical condition (the condition that hasn't been met) with the simple past tense. Use the main clause to express an imaginary situation with **would** + the base form of the main verb.

> If I **won** a million dollars, I **would buy** a big house.
>   Hypothetical condition   Imaginary situation

The meaning is that you don't have the million dollars so the house is a dream, not a reality. The whole situation is hypothetical.

A. Decide which situations will probably happen (✔) and which will probably not happen (✘).

1. If I had some correction fluid, I would change that word.
2. If I had more energy, I would play tennis more often.
3. If we stop spending so much money, we will not have so many debts.
4. If the student graduates this year, he will have a better chance of finding a job.
5. If he leaves the house half an hour earlier in the morning, he won't be late all the time.
6. If my mother cooks something special, I will invite you for dinner.
7. If I spoke more Japanese, I would understand the culture better.
8. If the weather doesn't improve, we will organize some indoor activities.
9. If she went to bed earlier, she wouldn't be so tired all the time.
10. If they had more friends, they wouldn't be so lonely.

Language in Transition

In present unreal (hypothetical) conditions where the verb in the main clause is **be**, the subjunctive form of the verb **be** is used in the **if** clause; i.e., **were** is used as the verb form with all persons and numbers (**if I were**, **if you were**, **if he were**, etc.). In informal conversations, it is common to use either the indicative or the subjunctive form: "If I **were** you, I would be careful" or "If I **was** you, I would be careful."

B. Complete the sentences with things you would like to do.

1. If we had longer summer holidays, we…
2. If I knew that girl's phone number, I…
3. If the exams were harder, some people…
4. If the climate were less damp and cold, we…

paper clips a highlighter a file folder a binder staples					
	26	27	28	29	30

5. If I got into debt, I…
6. If someone offered me an interesting job, I…
7. If everyone drove electric cars, we…
8. If big cities were less crowded, we…
9. If the whole world spoke one language, it…
10. If fewer people were greedy,…

Conditional II Negative Form

Either clause in a Conditional II sentence can be expressed in the negative.

If we weren't so tired, we would go dancing.
(We are tired so it is very unlikely that we will go dancing.)

If we were rich, **we wouldn't do** our own housework.
(We aren't rich so we probably do our own housework.)

Language in Transition

In formal language, Conditional II negative sentences use the subjunctive form **weren't**, but in informal language, the indicative form **wasn't** is often used.

A. Make one or both clauses negative so that the sentences will be logical.

If my neighbour was lazy, he would cut the grass.
If my neighbour wasn't so lazy, he would cut the grass.

1. If the weather were better, we would stay at home.
2. If English were difficult, we would learn it quickly.
3. If she were worried about her grades, she would be relaxed.
4. If the air were cleaner, we would have trouble with our health.
5. If all countries were peaceful, we would have conflict.
6. If I were busy, I would have time to socialize.
7. If you were sick, you would feel good.
8. If my life were hectic, I would have lots of free time.
9. If we were not in financial difficulties, we would have to spend less.
10. If they were impolite and selfish, they would have a lot of friends.

a 3-hole punch a recycling bin envelopes a waste basket thumb tacks					
	31	32	33	34	35

Conditional II Question Form

To form a question with Conditional II, use question word + **would** + subject + main verb.

A. Use your own ideas to complete the questions.

1. If you were a genius, what _____?
2. If you had the opportunity to travel, where _____?
3. If you had all the time in the world, how _____?
4. Where would you look if _____?
5. How would you communicate if _____?
6. If you didn't have to work, how _____?
7. If you had the chance to be someone else, who _____?
8. What would you eat if _____?
9. How would you survive if _____?
10. If you wanted to be totally alone, where _____?

UNDERSTAND: **Conditional III**

Use Conditional III (past unreal) for hypothetical or imaginary situations in the past. Use the **if** clause to express the hypothetical condition that didn't occur or wasn't met in past time using the past perfect form. Use the main clause to express the hypothetical or imaginary situation that did not occur with **would** + the base form of **have** + the past participle of the main verb.

If she **had studied** more, she would **have passed** the exam.

Past condition that didn't occur   Hypothetical situation that didn't occur

The meaning is that she didn't study and so the result is imaginary, rather than real. The whole situation is hypothetical or unreal.

Conditional III is often used to express either relief or regret about things that have never happened, and either have consequences in the present or had consequences in the past.

Regret: If I had studied harder, I would have had better marks.
(I didn't study hard enough and therefore I didn't have good marks.)

Relief: If the exam hadn't been so easy, we would have failed for sure.
(The exam was easy so we didn't fail.)

A. Match the sentences with the ones that follow.

We forgot about the appointment.

If you had entered the date in your electronic agenda, you wouldn't have forgotten it.

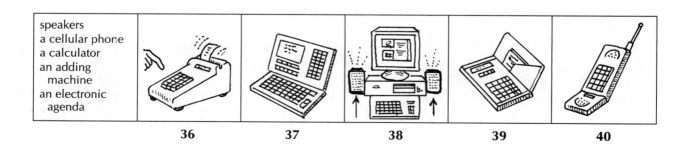

speakers a cellular phone a calculator an adding machine an electronic agenda				
36	37	38	39	40

1. I didn't know about his behaviour.
2. He didn't know the way.
3. She didn't have good study habits.
4. They did not provide good service.
5. She was only there for three days.
6. I didn't know about your plans.
7. They were poor administrators.
8. He tried to get into a well-known institution.
9. They couldn't afford food and accommodation any longer.
10. The cost of telephone calls was high.

a) If I had known that you were coming, I would have waited for you.
b) If he had applied to a less famous university, he would have been accepted.
c) They wouldn't have gone bankrupt if they had managed the company more efficiently.
d) If she had spent more time in Turkey, she would have visited you.
e) I wouldn't have asked him to come if I had known he was so rude.
f) If the hotels and restaurants hadn't been so expensive, they wouldn't have cut their vacation short.
g) He wouldn't have missed the lecture, if he hadn't got lost in the corridors.
h) If she had developed better study habits, she would have been a more successful student.
i) We would have called more often if the long distance rates had been lower.
j) We wouldn't have lost our tempers if the clerks hadn't been so slow and arrogant.

B. Complete the sentences with your own ideas.

If you had asked for information at the reception desk, you would have found the room more easily.

1. I would have had a better haircut if…
2. If I hadn't chosen such a hard course, I…
3. If she had only listened to me, she…
4. They would never have moved here if…
5. He wouldn't have seen the doctor if…
6. They wouldn't have retired if…
7. I would have travelled more if…
8. If he hadn't gotten sick, he…
9. If you had invited me to the party, I…
10. If no one had warned me, I…

a waiting room					
a briefcase					
a coat rack					
a reception area					
a conference room					
	41	42	43	44	45

Vocabulary Challenge

The Objects Quiz

What would you use in each of these situations? Choose the best answers.

1. If you wanted to file papers, you would use:
   a) a storeroom
   b) a stockroom
   c) a filing cabinet

2. If you wanted to correct a typing error, you would use:
   a) a highlighter
   b) a folder
   c) correction fluid

3. If you wanted to send a document to another office quickly, you would use:
   a) a photocopier
   b) a fax machine
   c) a typewriter

4. If you wanted to put some papers in a binder, you would use:
   a) a 3-hole punch
   b) a scanner
   c) thumbtacks

5. If you wanted to send a computer file, you would use:
   a) a monitor
   b) a modem
   c) a mouse

6. If your stapler was out of staples, you could use:
   a) paper clips
   b) thumbtacks
   c) a diskette

7. If you wanted to have a meeting, you could use:
   a) the reception area
   b) a waiting room
   c) a conference room

8. If you wanted to input data, you would use:
   a) a keyboard
   b) a typewriter
   c) a modem

9. If you wanted to keep business cards at your fingertips, you could use:
   a) file folders
   b) a rotary file
   c) a bulletin board

10. If you wanted to store stationery, you could use:
    a) a storeroom
    b) a stockroom
    c) a bulletin board

Ten-Minute Grammar Games

The Agony Column

Focus: Practise conditional sentences.

Students work in pairs or small groups. They write a short "Ann Landers"-type letter explaining a personal problem they are having.

Groups exchange letters and give advice, using as many conditional sentences as possible.

Students can then take turns reading their problems and solutions aloud.

Regrets

Focus: Practise conditional sentences.

Students work in pairs to write a dialogue. They choose or are assigned one of the following sets of roles:

- a) a husband and wife
- b) a girlfriend and boyfriend
- c) two good friends
- d) two co-workers

They must assume they have just had a disagreement, and are trying to patch things up. They write a dialogue, apologizing and expressing their regrets. They use as many conditional sentences as they can.

   If I hadn't _____ perhaps you wouldn't have _____ .

Students can then read their dialogues to the class. Other students try to guess their relationship and their problem.

Test Yourself

A. Complete the Conditional I sentences by putting the verbs in brackets in the correct tense.

1. If you don't go, everyone _____ (be) sad.
2. The party will not be a success if we _____ (not/have) music.
3. Rick won't serve meat, if you _____ (be) vegetarian.
4. If you don't work hard, you _____ (not/pass) the exam.
5. If Ana is in the garden, she _____ (not hear) the doorbell.
6. If he doesn't change his attitude, he _____ (not/be) successful.
7. We won't have the exam if the teacher _____ (be) absent.
8. Gaby will let us know if she _____ (not/get) an answer soon.
9. If you follow my advice, you _____ (not/have) any more problems.
10. If she doesn't understand me, I _____ (speak) more slowly.

B. Complete the Conditional II sentences by using the correct form of the verb in brackets.

1. If I _____ (get) into debt, I would cut up my credit cards.
2. He would buy a car, if he _____ (have) enough money.
3. We would understand better, if the teacher _____ (speak) more slowly.
4. If I _____ (ask) you for some money, would you lend it to me?
5. If she _____ (apply) to the college, she would get accepted.
6. Elena would win the race if she _____ (enter).
7. If he _____ (see) the announcement, would he apply for the job?
8. I would invest all the money if I _____ (win) the lottery.
9. They would get to class on time, if they _____ (have) a car.
10. If I _____ (know) him better, I would introduce you.
11. If he _____ (take) better care of himself, he would have fewer health problems.
12. If I _____ (know) how to skate, I would enjoy winter more.
13. They would save a lot of money on gas, if they _____ (drive) a smaller car.
14. She would be a better friend if she _____ (not/break) her promises.
15. If you _____ (live) in the city, you would get to work more quickly.

C. Complete the Conditional III sentences using the correct form of the verb in brackets.

1. If I had won the lottery, I _____ (quit) my job.
2. If we had used the computer to do our work, we _____ (finish) the job a lot sooner.
3. If my parents had spoken English when I was a child, I _____ (have) less trouble learning it as an adult.
4. If she had been born in a hot climate, she _____ (be) more tolerant of high temperatures.
5. If you had eaten less at the party, you _____ (feel) better afterwards.
6. If I had known what the problem was, I _____ (help) you with it.
7. If she had had more time to study, she _____ (get) higher marks.
8. If he had been a more serious student, he _____ (graduate) when he was supposed to.
9. If the weather had been more cooperative, we _____ (enjoy) our holiday more.
10. If they had driven a more reliable car, they _____ (arrive) when they were scheduled to.

D. Put the verbs in the correct tense.

1. If I had known it was so far, I _____ (not/go).
2. I will go to the meeting if I _____ (know) in advance.
3. I would work harder if you _____ (pay) me more money.
4. If I _____ (be) you, I wouldn't trust that guy.
5. I _____ (not/take) the picture if I had known there was no film in the camera.

Score for Test Yourself: _____

Vocabulary Answers

1. a photocopier	16. supplies	31. thumbtacks
2. a modem	17. letterhead	32. a wastebasket
3. a typewriter	18. a memo	33. a recycling bin
4. a fax machine	19. stationery	34. envelopes
5. a computer	20. a document	35. a 3-hole punch
6. a mouse	21. a stapler	36. an adding machine
7. a keyboard	22. a rotary file	37. an electronic agenda
8. a diskette	23. correction fluid	38. speakers
9. a monitor	24. a clipboard	39. a calculator
10. a printer	25. a business card	40. a cellular phone
11. a stockroom	26. a binder	41. a conference room
12. a storeroom	27. a file folder	42. a waiting room
13. a bulletin board	28. paper clips	43. a coat rack
14. a filing cabinet	29. staples	44. a briefcase
15. book shelves	30. a highlighter	45. a reception area

Modal Auxiliaries for Possibility and Probability
"Must" for Deduction
"Had better"

What Do You Know?

What Are They Talking About?

Match the pictures with the statements on page 90.

a

b

c

d

1. Be careful. It might be dangerous.
2. They must be going to a party.
3. The bus should be here any minute.
4. The weather report can't have been accurate.
5. She may be from the newspaper.
6. Their team must have won the game.
7. It might be for me.
8. You could have a broken leg.

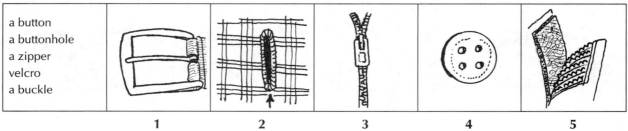

a button
a buttonhole
a zipper
velcro
a buckle

1   2   3   4   5

Understanding Grammar

UNDERSTAND: **Modal Auxiliary Verbs**

Modal auxiliary verbs are used to express possibility and probability or deduction and inference. Most modals have multiple functions depending on the context of use.

Modals are always put at the beginning of a verb phrase. Modals are followed by **the base form of the verb without to**. Only one modal can be used at a time.

> That skirt might be too small.
> We should learn that new dance before the party.

UNDERSTAND: **Expressing Possibility and Probability with Modals**

The modal **will** is used to express certainty. Some modals are used to express strong possibility or probability (**should, must**). Other modal auxiliaries are used to express possibility (**may, might, could**).

Certainty:	That magnificent painting **will** certainly win the prize.
High probability:	I hear a noise. There **must** be someone there.
	The bus is due. The bus **should** arrive any minute.
Possibility:	Someone is at the door. It **could** be Jack.
	I bought a ticket. I **may** win the raffle.
	I think they are out of town, but we can call anyway. They **might** be back by now.

a skirt
a shirt
seams
a waistband
pleats

6   7   8   9   10

A. Complete the following sentences with verbs from the list below.

become do arrive be remember know open take understand have

1. Ask for directions. Someone may _____ where the bus stop is.
2. Why don't we invite Sue? She should _____ free tonight.
3. Let's ask Edouard. He might _____ her telephone number.
4. Keep practising the violin. You could _____ famous one day.
5. Ask Alicia Gomez for help. She must _____ Spanish well.
6. Let's go to the bus station. Their bus should _____ soon.
7. Come to the other store. They might _____ lower prices on tights.
8. Let's get in line. The doors should _____ any minute now.
9. Don't worry about the math test. You may _____ better next time.
10. Ask Dan and Anna. They must _____ that train all the time.

Use the modal + the bare infinitive (without **to**) to express probability or possibility in present or future time with **should, could, may,** and **might**. **Must** cannot be used to express probability in future time.

Present: ✔ They **should** be back now.
          ✔ They **must** be back now.

Future: ✔ They **should** be back tomorrow.
          ✘ They **must** be back tomorrow.

Use the modal auxiliary + the base form of **have** + the past participle of the main verb to express probability or possibility in past time.

He **may have been** afraid.

Present or Future

I must
I should
I could   go
I may
I might

Past

I must
I should
I could   have gone
I may
I might

> **TEACHER'S BOX:** When **must** is used to refer to future time, the meaning is related to obligation rather than probability.
>
> Example: He must be back at work tomorrow (or he will be in trouble).

a collar a sleeve a cuff a hem belt loops		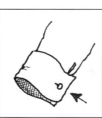	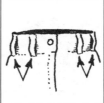	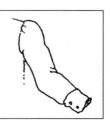	
	11	**12**	**13**	**14**	**15**

B. Change the verb phrases in these sentences to refer to past time.

He may be there. **He may have been there.**

1. They could be in the shoe department.
2. Everyone must be wearing fancy clothes.
3. Valery might win the dress-design competition.
4. The bus should leave at eight o'clock.
5. Michel may be the last one to arrive.
6. The Tangs could telephone after lunch.
7. The old sewing machine might break down under stress.
8. Someone could misunderstand the directions.
9. Anne should wear her turtleneck.
10. Their design must be the best in the fashion show.
11. Anyone could be elected to that committee.
12. They might forget to get off the bus.
13. There must be a better way to learn English.
14. Kathleen should win the fashion award.
15. You may be the best-dressed person at the party.

C. Match the sentences.

1. He studied really hard all term.
2. Hiroshi and Keiko missed the commuter train.
3. Maria can't find her glasses anywhere.
4. Peter got really sunburned yesterday.
5. Everyone looks grouchy today.
6. Several people in the class failed that exam.
7. Our hotel is somewhere in the neighbourhood.
8. I can't find the book I need in the bookstore.
9. Johnny had a stomachache at school yesterday.
10. Lili's hair looked shorter than it did the last time I saw her.

a) It might be the rainy weather.
b) She must have gone to the hairdresser.
c) It should be just around the corner.
d) They must have forgotten to set their alarm.
e) It might have been all the chocolate cake he ate.
f) You should find it in the public library.
g) He should have passed the exam without any difficulty.
h) He must have forgotten his sunscreen lotion.
i) It might have been too difficult for them.
j) She may have left them at home this morning.

a turtle-neck a crew neck a V-neck a hood tights					
	16	17	18	19	20

UNDERSTAND: **Negative Possibility with Modals**

To express negative possibility, use the modals **cannot (can't)**, **could not (couldn't)**, **may not**, and **might not**.

> There is no one home. This **can't** be the right address.
>
> It is only 5:15. They **might not** be home from work yet.

Use the negative form of the modal + the infinitive without **to** for present time. The modals **may not** and **might not** can also be used to express negative possibility in future time.

> They **might not** attend the reception tomorrow.
>
> They **may not** attend the reception tomorrow.

> **TEACHER'S BOX:** The modals **must** and **should** are not used to express negative possibility. The modals **cannot** and **could not** are not used to express future possibility. When they are used for future time, **cannot** and **could not** have a different meaning: "They can't attend the reception tomorrow" means that they are not able to attend it.

Use the negative form of the modal + **have been** to express negative possibility in the past.

> I saw him downtown. **He couldn't have been** at home last night.

A. Use the modal and the main verb to write the negative verb phrase in the past form.

could/wear   **could not have worn**

1. must/be	11. should/say
2. could/go	12. may/take
3. may/try	13. must/have
4. might/arrive	14. might/know
5. should/think	15. should/understand
6. could/leave	16. could/ride
7. may/eat	17. may/drive
8. must/write	18. must/grow
9. could/send	19. might/give
10. might/win	20. should/forget

a cardigan
a vest
a sweatshirt
a pocket
suspenders

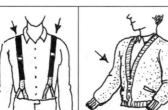

21	22	23	24	25

B. Read the situations below. Choose the conclusion that is the most probable for each one.

Mary works in a restaurant. She begins work at six in the morning. Because she has to be up so early, she always goes to bed early. It is one o'clock in the morning.

✔ (a) Mary couldn't be up at this hour.
(b) Mary might not be up at this hour.

1. People are waiting to get on the bus. They are wearing warm coats, boots, hats, gloves, and scarves. They are all shivering and looking unhappy.
   a) The temperature may be below zero.
   b) The temperature must be below zero.

2. Frank is weak in math. He skipped math class often and didn't study for the exam. The teacher is giving the exam results to the students in the math class today.
   a) Frank couldn't have a good mark.
   b) Frank shouldn't have a good mark.

3. The Wilson family was driving on the highway when suddenly their car stopped. The car had no mechanical problems so there was only one explanation.
   a) The car must have run out of gas.
   b) The car may have run out of gas.

4. Alexandra never leaves the office before six o'clock. It takes her about half an hour to get home. It is five-thirty and her room-mate is cooking dinner.
   a) Alexandra couldn't be home yet.
   b) Alexandra might not be home yet.

5. Johanna is leaving for a short holiday at the beach. Her neighbours see her drive up and begin unloading a large trunk from her car.
   a) It couldn't be for her trip to the beach.
   b) It shouldn't be for her trip to the beach.

6. People are arriving at work in a large office downtown. Everyone is dressed in business clothes. No one is wearing jeans, a sweatshirt, or loafers.
   a) It couldn't be "casual Friday."
   b) It may not be "casual Friday."

7. There is a violin competition that we really want to go to on the weekend. We were so busy we forgot to buy the tickets.
   a) It might not be too late.
   b) It could not be too late.

loafers sneakers sling backs pumps high heels					
	26	**27**	**28**	**29**	**30**

8. Someone brought a small birthday cake to the party. People at the party all had big pieces. Grace wants a piece of cake with her lunch today.
   a) There may not be any left.
   b) There couldn't be any left.

9. Our friends went to southern France on holiday in December. It was really cold and they had a miserable time. We are planning a holiday there in January.
   a) It might not be much warmer then.
   b) It should not be much warmer then.

10. Our course plan says that we have our class in the language lab on Tuesdays. Today we are practising pronunciation lessons in the language lab.
    a) It couldn't be Thursday today.
    b) It shouldn't be Thursday today.

UNDERSTAND: "Must" for Deductions

One use of the modal auxiliary **must** is to express deductions.

To express deductions in present time, use **must** before the bare infinitive.

   Janet stayed up till three in the morning. She **must** be tired.

To express deductions in past time, use **must** + the base form of **have** + the past participle of the main verb.

   Jason went to bed early yesterday. He **must have been** tired.

A. Write deductions based on the information given in brackets. Use **must** and present time.

   Ming isn't in class today. He was blowing his nose a lot yesterday. (sick)
   He must be sick.

   1. Mike just took two aspirins. (headache)
   2. Min Hee is yawning a lot. (sleepy)
   3. Marco ate a lot at dinner. (full)
   4. Hiroshi has big muscles. (a weightlifter)
   5. The dog is sitting near the door. (want to go outside)
   6. The tourists are looking at a map. (lost)
   7. Something is making me sneeze. (dust)
   8. Junko is coughing a lot. (a bad cold)
   9. Something smells good in the kitchen. (apple pie)
   10. Gaby is putting on sandals. (warm outside)

shoelaces a sole a heel a toe insoles				
31	32	33	34	35

11. The teacher is not in class. (absent)
12. The cat is meowing. (hungry)
13. Judy is putting on her sweater. (cold)
14. Tom doesn't want to come out tonight. (tired)
15. Suzy is wearing high heels. (want to be taller)

B. Write deductions using the information in brackets. Use **must** and the appropriate form of the verb.

Karen was wearing a bathing suit. (swim) **She must have been swimming.**

1. Everyone was wearing rubber boots. (rain)
2. Carlos was running for the bus. (late)
3. Lili and Chen weren't hungry. (their dinner)
4. Jack couldn't get into his car. (his keys)
5. Pablo had a cast on his arm. (an accident)
6. Franco was limping badly. (his foot)
7. Everyone there looked upset. (some bad news)
8. The lights at Randy's house were on. (at home)
9. Anne was stretching her muscles. (stiff)
10. Kwong and Jun were smiling. (some good news)
11. Francine looked very pale. (a ghost)
12. Nadia came to class late. (sleep in)
13. Martin woke up in the middle of the night. (noise)
14. Everything outside is white this morning. (snow)
15. The boss was late for the meeting yesterday. (busy)

overshoes rubbers rubber boots sandals moccasins					
	36	37	38	39	40

C. Look at the pictures and write deductions. Use **must** and the continuous form of the verb.

Example: **It must have been raining**

UNDERSTAND: "Had better"

The meaning of the phrase **had better** is similar to the meaning of **should** or **it is a good idea to do something**. **Had better** is used to express advisability in present or future time. It can be used in either the affirmative or negative form to offer advice.

> If you want to arrive on time, you'd better hurry up.
> If you want to arrive on time, you'd better not delay.

Use **had better** + the base form of the verb. Make the contraction with the subject pronoun + **'d**.

> We had better hurry.   **We'd** better hurry.

Use **had better** + **not** + the base form of the verb to form the negative of **had better**.

> We had better not go.   **We'd better not go**.

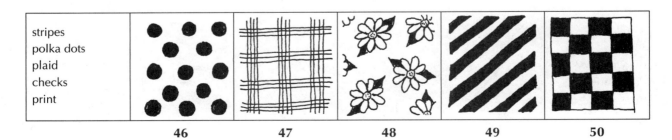

stripes polka dots plaid checks print					
	46	47	48	49	50

Full form	Contraction	Negative
I had better	I'd better	I had better not
you had better	you'd better	you had better not
he had better	he'd better	he had better not
she had better	she'd better	she had better not
it had better go	it'd better go	it had better not go
we had better	we'd better	we had better not
you had better	you'd better	you had better not
they had better	they'd better	they had better not

> **TEACHER'S BOX:** Although the phrase **had better** includes the past tense form of **had**, it refers to present and future time only.

A. Match the situations and advice using **had better**.

1. Mary is afraid she will feel sick on the plane.
2. It looks as though it might rain before we get back.
3. My car makes a terrible noise when I accelerate.
4. The police might stop us on the highway for speeding.
5. My hair is wet and I'm late for work.
6. Our refrigerator was almost empty the last time I looked.
7. A lot of people want to see that popular new play.
8. She has been complaining about back pain for quite a while.
9. Our dinner guests will be arriving in less than an hour.
10. Jim forgot to take the keys to his apartment twice last week.

a) We'd better go grocery shopping before we run out of everything.
b) She'd better try to make an appointment with the doctor right away.
c) We'd better get there early if we want to be sure to get tickets.
d) She'd better take some travel sickness medication before the flight.
e) We'd better remember to take our raincoats and umbrellas with us.
f) You'd better use a hair dryer so you can get ready more quickly.
g) We'd better begin setting the table and preparing the dinner right away.
h) We'd better slow down so we don't get a speeding ticket.
i) You'd better see a mechanic and have the muffler changed.
j) He'd better leave an extra set of house keys with the neighbours.

a hair dryer
a nail file
an emery board
a bobby pin
nail clippers

51   52   53   54   55

B. Choose the best verb to complete the sentence. Use the negative form of **had better**.

It's raining. We had better **not forget** our raincoats

forget try arrive go stay wear make speak eat play
spend ask for drive take get

1. Tom had better _____ too much money now or he won't have enough money next term.

2. If you are going to the beach today, you had better _____ out in the sun for too long.

3. If you want to improve your oral skills in English, you had better _____ your own language too much.

4. The restaurant we want to go to is very popular. We'd better _____ late or they won't hold our reservations.

5. Our neighbours are very fussy. We'd better _____ any noise after eleven o'clock.

6. The children have a lot of cavities in their teeth. They'd better _____ any candy.

7. He's been sick all night with the flu. He had better _____ to work today.

8. The roads are very slippery tonight. You had better _____ anywhere this evening.

9. If you are going to drive such a long distance, you had better _____ your old car.

10. It is going to be very cold this evening. You had better _____ to take a warm coat.

11. People had better _____ swimming in the ocean because there is a report of sharks.

12. Francisco had better _____ soccer today because he suffered an injury in the last game.

13. Poling had better _____ a part-time job because she has a lot of courses to study for.

14. Your watch band is torn. You had better _____ your watch or you may lose it.

15. Normand is late for work again. He had better _____ any favours from the supervisor today.

a watch band a bracelet a chain a necklace beads				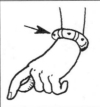	
	56	57	58	59	60

Vocabulary Challenge

What Will You Wear?

Put these words into categories. You should have nine groups of three words each.

bracelet   bathrobe   buttons   chain   checked   collar   crew neck   cuff   emery board
heel   high heels   nail clipper   nail file   necklace   nightgown   polka dots   pumps
pyjamas   sleeve   sling backs   sole   striped   toe   turtle-neck   V-neck   velcro   zipper

Ten-Minute Grammar Games

Solve the Problems

Focus: Practise modal auxiliaries.

1. Nancy and Robert are running in a race from the park to the sports stadium. Robert begins running at 2:00, and Nancy begins at 3:00. At the moment they run past each other, who must be closer to the stadium?

2. Ben wakes up very early in the morning to go jogging. One morning he gets up before sunrise. When he tries to turn on the light, he realizes that the light bulb has burned out. He knows that he has 12 pairs of blue socks and 12 pairs of black socks in his drawer, but he can't tell which is which. How many socks had he better pull out to find a matching set? How many had he better pull out to find a blue set?

Test Yourself

A. Choose the correct form of the verb to complete the sentences.

1. Jerome was late for the meeting. He _____ (must/be) held up in the office.
2. Gino hasn't arrived yet. He _____ (may/forget) the address of the building.
3. The bus is a little late this morning. It _____ (should/be) here any minute.
4. Peter is never late. Something _____ (must/happen) to hold him up.
5. I'm worried about the weather. Some people _____ (may/stay) at home because of it.
6. Gabrielle hasn't arrived yet. She _____ (might/miss) the train she was supposed to take.
7. Franco and Tony aren't here yet. They _____ (should/arrive) within the hour.
8. Junko and Keiko aren't here yet. They _____ (may/be) lost somewhere in the city.
9. Maria is late for work. She _____ (must/sleep in) this morning.
10. The tourist guide is smiling. He _____ (could/have) some good news to announce.

B. Look at the situations. Change the verbs in bold type to the negative form to make the information logical. Make changes to the verb tense if necessary.

I couldn't find my keys. **I may have put** them in my bag. **I may not have put them in my bag.**

1. Bin wasn't there at the time. Her information **might be** correct.
2. Tony **could make** that delicious cake. He doesn't know how to cook.
3. Mei-Ling didn't introduce us. She **may remember** all of our names.
4. Simon lived just across the street. He **should be** late for class.
5. We mailed the postcards from Rome. They **could be** postmarked Venice.
6. Those two musicians **might come** from the same region. They really played a different kind of music.
7. Patricia **may arrive** on time. She had to work until six o'clock last night.
8. He didn't seem to know that it was raining. He **could be** outside this morning.
9. Those two seemed uncomfortable together. They **may meet** before.
10. Suzanna didn't write in her notebook last class. She **might bring** it with her.

C. Complete the sentences with **must** + verb or **must have** + verb.

1. Tony and Pat kept yawning at the dinner table. They _____ (be) really tired.
2. My sister really ate a lot at dinner last night. She _____ (feel) pretty hungry.
3. Louise has a box of tissues on her desk. She _____ (have) quite a bad cold.
4. Motorists are driving very carefully today. There _____ (be) a lot of ice on the road.
5. Robert is wearing a cast on his leg today. He _____ (break) it when he fell down.
6. Karina bought quite a few lottery tickets. She _____ (want) to win really badly.
7. Those plants haven't grown very much. They _____ (need) more sun or water.
8. Nobody is at the stadium at the moment. They _____ (postponed) the game until another time.
9. That car has a parking ticket on the windshield. The meter _____ (run out) of time.
10. You are shivering. You _____ (be) out in the snow storm.

D. Make a logical sentence with the verb in brackets by choosing the affirmative or negative form of **had better**.

It's very cold out today. **I had better (wear) a hat.**

1. My wallet has just been stolen. I'd better _____ (report) it to the police immediately.
2. The computer I bought last week is defective. I'd better _____ (take) it back to the store right away.
3. I was late twice this week for an important meeting. I'd better _____ (be) late again or I might lose my job.

104

4. My biology teacher is so boring that I fell asleep in class. I'd better _____ (fall asleep) again or he'll be angry.

5. I missed my dentist appointment last week. I'd better _____ (miss) one again or she might charge me.

6. I have to finish my research paper this weekend. I'd better _____ (spend) the whole weekend at the library.

7. The doctor thinks I may have heart problems. I'd better _____ (stop) smoking right away.

8. I'm trying to lose weight. I'd better _____ (have) desserts anymore.

9. I've been working seven days a week for the last few months. I'd better _____ (take) some time off.

10. I forgot my sister's birthday last year. I'd better _____ (forget) it again this year.

Score for Test Yourself: _____
40

Vocabulary Answers

1. a buckle	21. suspenders	41. boxer shorts
2. a buttonhole	22. a cardigan	42. a nightgown
3. a zipper	23. a vest	43. pyjamas
4. a button	24. a sweatshirt	44. a bathrobe
5. velcro	25. a pocket	45. slippers
6. seams	26. sling backs	46. polka dots
7. a skirt	27. pumps	47. plaid
8. pleats	28. high heels	48. print
9. a shirt	29. sneakers	49. stripes
10. a waistband	30. loafers	50. checks
11. a hem	31. a toe	51. an emery board
12. a collar	32. insoles	52. nail clippers
13. a cuff	33. shoelaces	53. a nail file
14. belt loops	34. a heel	54. a hair dryer
15. a sleeve	35. a sole	55. a bobby pin
16. a crew-neck	36. sandals	56. a necklace
17. a V-neck	37. rubbers	57. a watch band
18. a turtle-neck	38. moccasins	58. beads
19. tights	39. rubber boots	59. a bracelet
20. a hood	40. overshoes	60. a chain

9

Direct Speech
Indirect Speech
"Say" and "Tell"

What Do You Know?

Who Said What?

Read the joke. Then practise telling it to your partner. After class, tell the joke to someone else.

Stop Swearing

A man bought a parrot in a pet shop. When he got home, the parrot began to swear. The man said, "Stop that!", but the parrot continued to swear. Finally the man decided to call the pet shop. "What can I do?" he asked the pet shop owner. "This parrot won't stop swearing."

"Here's what to do. Put the parrot in the fridge for five minutes. When it comes out, it won't swear anymore," the pet shop owner said. "OK, I'll try it," the man replied. He put the parrot in the fridge and explained, "This is because you are swearing." Then he shut the fridge door and went away.

Five minutes later he returned and opened the door. The poor parrot was shivering and shaking. "Do you promise never to swear again?" asked the man. "Oh yes, I promise," said the bird. Then the parrot continued, "I'll never swear again, but I have a question for you." "What's the question?" the man asked. "The chicken," said the parrot, "what did **it** do?"

Understanding Grammar

UNDERSTAND: **Direct Speech**

Use direct speech to report what someone else said using the speaker's exact words. Direct speech is generally used in story telling, fiction, and newspaper and magazine writing.

To show that you are using direct speech, use a comma after the introductory verb, and quotation marks on either side of the speaker's actual words.

> My grandfather always says, "Anyone can learn to play the piccolo."

Some verbs that are commonly used to introduce direct speech describe how statements are spoken: **say**, **sigh**, **laugh**, **shout**, **cry**, etc. Others show the purpose of the speaker's words: **answer**, **reply**, **continue**, **explain**, **comment**, etc.

TEACHER'S BOX: The verb **tell** is not used to introduce direct speech.

✔ She said, "Hi."

✘ She told (me), "Hi."

A. Punctuate the following sentences correctly.

Shakespeare said to be or not to be.

Shakespeare said, "To be, or not to be?"

1. Neil Armstrong said one small step for man one giant step for mankind.
2. Albert Einstein said energy equals mass times the speed of light squared.
3. Ann Landers said people who drink to drown their sorrows should be told that sorrows know how to swim.
4. A well-known proverb says never put off until tomorrow what you can do today.
5. A famous bumper sticker says don't follow me I'm lost.
6. Benjamin Disraeli said the reason you have one mouth and two ears is so you can listen twice as much as you talk.
7. Confucius said to know the road ahead ask someone who is coming back.
8. Victor Hugo said no army can stop an idea whose time has come.
9. An Arabian proverb says if the camel gets its nose in the tent its body will soon follow.
10. Al Capone once said I don't even know what street Canada is on.

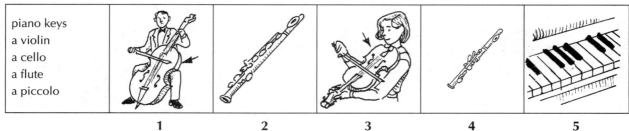

piano keys a violin a cello a flute a piccolo					
	1	2	3	4	5

B. Match the introductory statements with the words that probably followed them.

1. The teacher said
2. The doctor advised
3. The coach threatened
4. The flight attendant said
5. The head nurse asked
6. The tourist inquired
7. The angry policeman shouted
8. The taxi driver asked
9. The travel agent explained
10. The personnel officer asked

a) Anyone who is caught smoking will be off the team.
b) Lower seat rates are in effect as of next week.
c) Smoking has been shown to contribute to cancer.
d) You may turn over your papers and begin the exam now.
e) Show me your driver's licence and registration.
f) Where would you like to go?
g) Please make sure your seat belts are fastened securely.
h) Is there anyone here who can work a double shift today?
i) Is this the right bus for the Eiffel Tower?
j) Do you have any experience in international law?

C. Write the sentences above out as direct speech with appropriate punctuation.

The music teacher said, "It is hard to learn to play the organ."

UNDERSTAND: **Indirect Speech**

Use indirect speech to report what a speaker said without using his or her exact words. Use **that** after the reporting verb to introduce the speaker's words.

The teacher **said that**...

TEACHER'S BOX: When **tell** is used as the reporting verb, it must be followed by a direct object: "He **told us** that he was tired."

---

a guitar drums an organ a harmonica an accordion					
	6	7	8	9	10

Several grammatical changes are common when reporting with indirect speech. These can be classified as verb changes, adverbial changes, and pronoun changes.

Verb Changes

When reporting with indirect speech, verbs move one tense to the past:

present to past
present continuous to past continuous
present perfect to past perfect
past to past perfect
can to **could**
may to **might**
will to **would**

"I **study** music."   She said that she **studied** music.
"I **will see** you soon."   He said that he **would see** us soon.

A. Change the sentences to indirect speech with **that** and the appropriate change of tense.

The policeman said, "The road through the mountains is unsafe."
The policeman said that the road through the mountains was unsafe.

1. The artist said, "Water colours are easy to use."
2. The teacher said, "The exam tomorrow will be difficult."
3. John said, "People don't like the idea of getting home late."
4. Angela said, "Tourists can't find the bus station easily."
5. The ringmaster said, "The acrobats will ride on the elephants."
6. The driver said, "The bus won't go until everyone is on board."
7. Mrs. Tang said, "The weather was terrible in England."
8. The tourist said, "Paris is a beautiful city to visit."
9. Mr. Dupont said, "The musicians aren't going to be happy in an old concert hall."
10. The conductor said, "Everyone needs to tune their instruments."
11. An actress said, "The theatre is the highest form of art."
12. The singer said, "Not everyone will agree with that statement."
13. My teacher said, "Students everywhere are the same."
14. Francisco said, "Everyone really enjoyed the performance."
15. Mary said, "Cats don't generally like water very much."

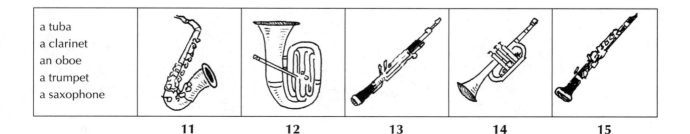

a tuba
a clarinet
an oboe
a trumpet
a saxophone

11   12   13   14   15

Adverbial Changes

In indirect speech, adverbials and demonstratives become more distant in time and space:

here to **there**
now to **then**
this/these to **that/those**
this night to **that night**
tonight to **that night**
next morning to **the following morning**
tomorrow to **the following day**
yesterday to **the day before**

A. Change the sentences to indirect speech. Make changes to the verbs. Make changes to the adverbials or demonstratives in brackets.

I said, "I don't want to paint (here)."
I said that I didn't want to paint there.

1. I said, "I think the piano is out of tune (tonight)."
2. We said, "We really enjoyed the party (yesterday)."
3. I said, "I don't want to park my car near (this one)."
4. My boss and I said, "We plan to open a factory (here next year)."
5. We said, "We can change places (tomorrow morning)."
6. My fiancé and I said, "We are going to be married (next year)."
7. I said, "I am going to buy (this) car (tomorrow)."
8. I said, "I am taking tuba lessons (here now)."
9. Jim and I said, "We have studied saxophone (here) for six months."
10. I said, "I will meet you (next week)."

Pronoun Changes

In indirect speech, pronouns change from first to third person (unless the reporter and the speaker are the same person).

He said, "I have lost my dictionary."
He said that he had lost his dictionary.

bagpipes a tambourine a musician a concert hall a stage				
	16	17	18	19	20

A. Put the correct pronouns in the following sentences.

1. The doctor said, "You should stop smoking cigarettes."
The doctor said that _____ should stop smoking cigarettes.

2. My friend and I said, "He looks like a good juggler."
My friend and I said that _____ looked like a good juggler.

3. They said, "You should see if you can rent a car."
They said that _____ should see if _____ could rent a car.

4. She said, "I would really like to join your circus."
She said that _____ would really like to join _____ circus.

5. Mike and Bob said, "Everyone gets along well in our orchestra."
Mike and Bob said that everyone got along well in _____ orchestra.

6. Someone said, "You should hang your coat in the closet."
Someone said that _____ should hang _____ coat in the closet.

7. Everyone says, "You should all register early for that course."
Everyone says that _____ should register early for that course.

8. Maria announced, "I am sick of using charcoal and ink to draw."
Maria announced that _____ was sick of using charcoal and ink to draw.

9. The letter carrier said, "I'm sorry. There are no letters for you and me."
The letter carrier said that _____ was sorry that there were no letters for
_____ .

10. The magician said, "You have to see what I can pull out of my hat."
The magician said that _____ had to see what he could pull out of _____
hat.

B. Change the sentences to indirect speech. Make all the necessary changes.

She said, "I want to leave now."
She said that she wanted to leave then.

1. They replied, "It is too cold here."
2. Maria replied, "I have seen enough of this movie."
3. My boss announced, "Anyone who is late will be fired."
4. The hungry teenager complained, "I want to eat something now."
5. Their mother said, "It is too late to watch TV now."

a conductor an orchestra an orchestra pit sheet music a baton				
	21	22	23	24	25

6. The conductor said, "We can all fit onto this stage easily."
7. The tour guide said, "You will be late if you don't leave for the play now."
8. Our boss announced, "Employees are not allowed to park here without permits."
9. Someone suggested, "You should leave here tonight."
10. Mike said, "I think everyone should leave here tomorrow."

UNDERSTAND: **Questions in Indirect Speech**

Yes/No Questions

To report on yes/no questions in indirect speech, put the reporting verb in the past tense and replace that with **whether** or **if**. Do not use question-form word order in indirect speech (inversion of subject and verb). Do not use a question mark.

Ann asked, "Am I on time?"
Ann asked whether she was on time.

A. Report on the following yes/no questions using indirect speech.

1. Are we on time for the concert? (My aunt asked)
2. Is this the train for New York? (The tourist inquired)
3. Are these jackets on sale today? (Suzanne asked)
4. Is the violin out of tune? (My grandmother asked)
5. Is this the best work the class can do? (The teacher)
6. Is there another movie we can watch? (My friend)
7. Are we next-door neighbours? (The man I met in the hall)
8. Are you and your brother twins? (The math teacher)
9. Are there any more lions in the cage? (The lion tamer)
10. Is that an oil painting? (My mother-in-law)

WH-Questions

To report on WH-questions in indirect speech, put the reporting verb in the past tense and use the question word to indicate that you are reporting a question. Do not use question-form word order (inversion of subject and verb) in indirect speech. Do not use a question mark.

Why are they late?"
Someone asked why they were late.

a canvas a sketch pad charcoal ink a sculpture					
	26	27	28	29	30

A. Report on these questions in indirect speech.

The clown asked, "Who is this?"

The clown asked who that was.

1. The tourist wondered, "When does the next bus leave?"
2. My friend asked, "How long is the trip to Boston?"
3. The grouch asked, "Why is there such a long delay?"
4. The magician asked, "Where did I put my rabbit?"
5. The desk clerk asked, "What time will they arrive?"
6. The club president asked, "When can we get together?"
7. The visitor asked, "What does that sign mean?"
8. The doctor asked, "How have you been feeling?"
9. Susan asked, "What is this delicious cake made of?
10. The new employee asked, "How often do I need to wear a tie?

UNDERSTAND: **Imperatives in Indirect Speech**

Affirmative Imperative

Use the infinitive form of the verb to report imperative statements in indirect speech.

Teacher (to us): "Come in."
The teacher asked us **to come in**.

A. Change the reports of imperative statements into indirect speech.

The coach told us, "Pass the ball farther."

The coach told us to pass the ball farther.

1. The mother ordered the naughty children, "Go to bed!"
2. The police officer ordered the burglar, "Come out of the basement."
3. One student asked another student, "Pass the pencil sharpener."
4. Our teacher advised us, "Check the answers carefully."
5. The bank teller told me, "Please sign the back of the cheque."
6. The radio announcer advised the public, "Be careful of the water."
7. The father told his son, "Be home by eleven o'clock, or else."
8. The bank robber told the teller, "Hand over the cash quickly."
9. The teacher told the students, "Wait in the corridor."
10. The art student told her sister, "Leave my paintbrushes alone."

an easel a paintbrush a frame oil paint a palette				
	31	32	33	34	35

Negative Imperative

Use **not** + infinitive with **to** for reporting negative imperatives in indirect speech.

> The teacher told the students, "Don't talk."
> The teacher told the student **not to talk**.

A. Write sentences using the negative imperative for reporting with indirect speech.

1. The ringmaster told the audience, "Don't be afraid!"
2. The usher warned the people buying tickets, "Don't be late for the concert."
3. Sylvie told her friends, "Don't worry about anything."
4. The doctor advised the woman, "Don't smoke."
5. The conductor warned the violinist, "Don't play too fast."
6. Mario told his brother, "Don't use the bike without asking."
7. The police officer told the driver, "Don't turn left at the corner."
8. Keiko told her family, "Don't send any letters after June 1."
9. Pierre told his wife, "Don't forget to buy gas on the way home."
10. Everyone advised us, "Don't go to Hawaii in the summer."

UNDERSTAND: **"Say" and "Tell"**

The most common reporting verbs are **say** and **tell**. Use **say** (said) for direct speech or when there is no mention of the person to whom the speaker was talking.

> He said that he was tired.

Use **tell** (**told**) for indirect speech when mentioning the person **to whom the speaker was talking**.

> He told **me** that he was tired.

A. Change the verb **say** to **tell** and identify the person who was spoken to. Use the correct tense.

> He said that it was late. (his friend)
> **He told his friend that it was late.**

1. The speaker said that a cure for the disease could be found in about ten years. (the audience)
2. The computer salesman said that the model she wanted to buy was obsolete. (the customer)

a clown a lion tamer a trapeze artist a contortionist a magician					
	36	**37**	**38**	**39**	**40**

3. The psychologist said that this form of behaviour was generally easy to modify. (the patient)

4. The hostess said that coffee would be served in the living room after dinner. (the guests)

5. The police chief said that crime had decreased in certain neighbourhoods. (the journalists)

6. The professor said that the research project would have to be at least 20 pages long. (the students)

7. The sales manager said that the new styles would be in by the following week. (the sales representatives)

8. The film director said that the movie would be sure to make millions of dollars. (the actress)

9. The adoption agency said that the baby would be available in two months time. (the couple)

10. The teacher said that there would be a very difficult exam and that they should study hard. (the students)

B. Complete the sentences by adding a suitable person or animal from the list below.

**the juggler   the children   his mother   the cat   the passengers
the soldier   her room-mate   the visitors   the customers   the teacher**

1. He told _____ that he wouldn't be home for dinner.
2. She told _____ to get off the table immediately.
3. The bus driver told _____ that the bus had engine failure.
4. The waiter told _____ that the dessert they wanted wasn't on the menu.
5. They told _____ they had forgotten their dictionaries at home.
6. The sergeant told _____ to obey orders or face discipline hearings.
7. The student told _____ to get another apartment next semester.
8. The tour guide told _____ to have their passports ready for customs.
9. The ringmaster told _____ to get his act together.
10. The day-care teacher told _____ to wash their hands before lunch.

an acrobat a juggler a circus tent stilts a ringmaster					
	41	42	43	44	45

Vocabulary Challenge

Arts and Entertainment: Who Said It?

Complete the sentences, using the words you have learned from the picture dictionary.

1. "I broke my string" said the _____ .
2. "I've lost my baton" said the _____ .
3. "Get that rabbit out of my hat" said the _____ .
4. "My make-up isn't quite right" said the _____ .
5. "I'm all tied up" said the _____ .
6. "I'm in the pits" said the _____ .
7. "These keys are out of tune" said the _____ .
8. "Let's meet in the middle" said one _____ to another.
9. "It's not easy keeping everything in the air" said the _____ .
10. "I love working with wild animals" said the _____ .

Arts and Entertainment: What Am I?

1. "I'm a string instrument that begins with 'C.' I'm a _____ ."
2. "I'm an instrument with black and white keys. I'm a _____ ."
3. "I am something that people use to paint on. I'm a _____ ."
4. "When people play by ear, they don't need me. I'm _____ ."
5. "I'm a small instrument that people can carry in their pockets. I'm a _____ ."
6. "The conductor waves me around. I'm a _____ ."
7. "I am black and dusty. People draw with me. I'm _____ ."
8. "I'm a small wind instrument that begins with 'F.' I'm a _____ ."
9. "I'm big, and I make a loud boom. I'm a _____ ."
10. "I keep a picture in its place. I'm a _____ ."

Ten-Minute Grammar Games

Medieval Puzzles

Focus: Practise direct speech.

Students look at the pictures and choose the quotations on page 117 that probably go with them.

1. "Oh, oh. It looks like the ladder broke."
2. "I told him not to take a third helping at dinner."
3. "I hope she doesn't get a surprise when she looks inside."
4. "What do you mean, attack the castle? I haven't finished playing admirals yet."
5. "Are you sure I'll lose weight if I drink this stuff twice a day?"
6. "How long do I have to stay like this?"

A Soap Opera

Focus: Practise direct and indirect speech.

Students work in pairs to write a scene for a soap opera. They can use the beginning provided below, or write a new one of their own. They should use a mixture of direct and indirect speech.

> Joey was in love with Veronica, but Veronica didn't love Joey. Joey called Veronica every day. When Veronica's mother answered the phone, she told Veronica that it was Joey, and that he wanted to speak to her. Veronica always answered "Tell him I'm busy." Then one day…

After students have written their scenes, they can take turns reading them to the class.

Test Yourself

A. Change the statements into direct speech. Make all the necessary changes.

We said that it was time to go.
We said, "It is time to go."

1. The doctor said that the patient needed to be hospitalized.
2. The newscaster reported that the forest fire was under control.
3. The meteorologist announced that there was a tornado warning.
4. The bank manager said that interest rates would go up that week.
5. The ballet teacher said that everyone needed to practise more.
6. The photographer said that he needed to take more pictures.
7. The police officer said that we needed to fasten our seat belts.
8. The officer manager said that the new computer system would be installed soon.
9. The air-traffic controller said that some flights would be delayed.
10. The fashion designer said the autumn styles were exceptional that year.

B. Change the sentences into indirect speech. Make all the necessary changes.

She said, "It is late."
She said that it was late.

1. They said, "We have been to Europe before."
2. He answered, "A two-way ticket will be cheaper."
3. The guide explained, "We will have to wait for our turn."

4. They said, "They will try to take better care next time."
5. She said, "The party is going to be a big hit."
6. The teenagers promised, "We will be home before 11:00."
7. Our teacher explained, "You will all pass if you study hard."
8. They said, "We are too tired to do any more work."
9. He said, "The water is too cold to swim in."
10. They said, "We have to be home in time for dinner."

C. Change the imperative statements into indirect speech with **they said**. Make any necessary changes.

"Don't add salt until you have tasted the food."

They said not to add salt until we had tasted the food.

1. "Turn right at the street corner."
2. "Don't cross the street without looking."
3. "Don't worry about the math exam."
4. "Remember to bring your passport when you come here."
5. "Try to guess, if you aren't sure of the answer."
6. "Wait until other passengers have left the aircraft."
7. "Don't forget to brush your teeth before you go to bed."
8. "Don't forget to turn off the lights before you leave."
9. "Check the price before you buy these peaches."
10. "Help yourselves to anything you see here."

D. Choose **say** or **tell** and put it in the appropriate tense.

1. He _____ me not to worry about what had happened.
2. I always _____ what I think, no matter what people say.
3. John _____ the doctor that he felt sick after dinner.
4. Some people _____ that time has the same value as money.
5. He usually _____ people what he thinks about things.
6. They _____ us that the train would arrive late.
7. Someone _____ that the train would not be on time.
8. Everyone _____ us that it would not be a good idea to go.
9. People _____ that you shouldn't believe everything you hear.
10. She _____ me that it was a good idea to shop here.

Score for Test Yourself: _____

Vocabulary Answers

1. a cello	16. a musician	31. oil paint
2. a flute	17. bagpipes	32. a frame
3. a violin	18. a stage	33. a palette
4. a piccolo	19. a tambourine	34. an easel
5. piano keys	20. a concert hall	35. a paintbrush
6. drums	21. sheet music	36. a contortionist
7. a harmonica	22. a baton	37. a trapeze artist
8. an accordion	23. a conductor	38. a magician
9. an organ	24. an orchestra pit	39. a clown
10. a guitar	25. an orchestra	40. a lion tamer
11. a saxophone	26. ink	41. stilts
12. a tuba	27. a sketch pad	42. a circus tent
13. an oboe	28. a sculpture	43. a ringmaster
14. a trumpet	29. a canvas	44. an acrobat
15. a clarinet	30. charcoal	45. a juggler

10 Review Unit

TOEFL® Practice Exercises

You have 25 minutes to complete these exercises. When you complete Part A, continue to Part B. An answer sheet is provided on page 195.

Part A

Choose the phrase that best completes the sentence. Blacken the letter that corresponds to your answer on the answer sheet.

Example: A university spokesperson said that one of the objectives _____ the pleasures of student life without the problems associated with alcohol.

     (a) is to maintain
     (b) was to maintain
     (c) was maintained
     (d) is maintaining

        (A) (B) (C) (D)

1. While people in the audience were listening to the final song in the concert, _____ the sky to see if it was going to rain.
  (a) they were looking
  (b) they are looking at
  (c) they looks at
  (d) they were looking at

2. _____, you will see the ghosts of women knitting on their balconies and a cat sneaking under the fence.
  (a) If you look hard enough
  (b) If you looking hard enough
  (c) If you will look hard enough
  (d) If you looked hard enough

3. I was really bored during that film, and when I looked around me in the theatre I realized that _____ everyone else.
   - (a) either was
   - (b) so was
   - (c) neither were
   - (d) neither was

4. The tour guide _____ all the visitors to meet her in front of the famous opera house at two o'clock.
   - (a) said
   - (b) told to
   - (c) told
   - (d) tell

5. John has been playing chess all his life so he _____ be an expert, but he is still a rather mediocre player.
   - (a) should
   - (b) must
   - (c) can
   - (d) will

6. Robert seems to be coming down with a lot of colds and he has been told that he _____ taking care of himself before he becomes seriously ill.
   - (a) should better start
   - (b) had better start
   - (c) is better starting
   - (d) is better to start

7. _____ there is a lot of traffic or some other unexpected delay, they should be home before dinner.
   - (a) Because
   - (b) If
   - (c) So
   - (d) Unless

8. Inexperienced managers are not always able to figure out what their priorities _____ .
   - (a) can be
   - (b) would be
   - (c) should be
   - (d) has to be

9. If it _____, they will have to postpone the baseball game they are planning for tomorrow.
   - (a) rained
   - (b) could rain
   - (c) would rain
   - (d) rains

10. More students will understand the lecture if the teaching assistant _____ more slowly and more clearly next time.
    (a) will speak
    (b) would speak
    (c) spoke
    (d) speaks

11. If we don't take the opportunity to _____ the environment now, we will come to regret it deeply later on.
    (a) become involved to protect
    (b) become involved to protecting
    (c) become involved in protecting
    (d) became involved in protection

12. The accident _____ if they had been more careful when they installed the new machinery in the factory.
    (a) can has been prevented
    (b) will have been prevented
    (c) could have been prevented
    (d) wouldn't have been prevented

13. If more subsidized housing were available, there _____ so many homeless people in the city.
    (a) would be
    (b) could be
    (c) could not be
    (d) would not be

14. Joanne is a very unrealistic person who always _____ she had things that are impossible for her to get.
    (a) hopes
    (b) wishes
    (c) wants
    (d) would like

15. If interest rates in this country _____ lower, more people would borrow money to buy new houses.
    (a) were
    (b) would be
    (c) was
    (d) are

124

Part B

One of the underlined grammar points in each sentence is incorrect. Blacken the number of the error on the answer sheet.

Example: Before <u>his defeat</u>^A in the last election, the mayor <u>has approved</u>^B an expenditure of <u>many</u>^C millions of dollars <u>on</u>^D a sewage treatment plant.

(A) (B) (C) (D)

16. It <u>had turned</u>^A chilly by eight o'clock, but I <u>have stood</u>^B and shivered because I <u>wanted to</u>^C see the aurora borealis for <u>the</u>^D first time.

17. The jewellery store owner said that the gunman <u>was planned</u>^A the robbery very <u>well</u>^B and knew exactly <u>what</u>^C time the store <u>closed</u>^D.

18. The trial <u>was stopped</u>^A when the accused said he <u>couldn't</u>^B no longer defend <u>himself</u>^C and needed <u>to consult</u>^D a lawyer.

19. If that <u>had happened</u>^A, the <u>musician's</u>^B life a century and a quarter later would <u>have took</u>^C an <u>entirely</u>^D different turn.

20. The police said that an older man <u>had been</u>^A detained <u>in</u>^B the case <u>on</u>^C charges of <u>spread</u>^D false rumours about the government.

21. I <u>had forgotten</u>^A to prepare <u>my</u>^B classes and <u>it</u>^C was the longest day I had <u>never</u>^D put in as a teacher in the classroom.

22. If you <u>head</u>^A towards the east coast of India, <u>there is</u>^B a chance <u>of see</u>^C the eclipse <u>for up to</u>^D two minutes.

23. Climatologists <u>told to</u>^A us that it <u>was</u>^B the hottest summer the world <u>had seen</u>^C in 100 years—as if anyone around here <u>hadn't</u>^D noticed.

24. We <u>should remembered</u>^A the origins of <u>such</u>^B beliefs, and take <u>them</u>^C seriously instead of <u>countering</u>^D with threats and ridicule.

25. People <u>said</u>^A that they <u>wouldn't</u>^B have done it if they <u>had not been force</u>^C to <u>by</u>^D the nature of the competition.

26. A candidate for membership <u>must has</u>^A a skill <u>that</u>^B the other members of the organization feel <u>will be</u>^C useful <u>to them</u>^D.

27. <u>It is called</u>^A the Dream Flight, and <u>since</u>^B February the airline employees <u>has been</u>^C working day and night <u>getting</u>^D it off the ground.

28. Buzz Aldrin said at the press conference th**A**at he hoped his science **B** fiction book wou**C**ld be ma**D**ke into a series of movies.

29. If you will del**A**ete a file, you may **B** think that it is go**C**ne forever, but it may be possible to **D** get it back.

30. If he hadn't bei**A**ng such a capable driver, he could **B** not have avoided the onco**C**ming car at the speed it was trave**D**lling.

31. T**A**he hurricane may has **B** blown in a new species of caterpillar th**C**at was previously unkno**D**wn on that particular island.

32. The bus was so **A** late arriving that in the **B** time it got there almost everyone ha**C**d finished eating dinner and was wa**D**tching TV.

33. The coach remi**A**nded the players o**B**n the high school basketball team that they did **C** not win a si**D**ngle game in the whole season.

34. If science will eve**A**r discover a gene that can de**B**termine who will beco**C**me a criminal later in life, the scientific community will **D** be astonished.

35. The teacher told **A** to the anxious students th**B**at the literature exam they woul**C**d have on Thursday woul**D**d be very difficult.

36. The planetarium coordinator told **A** to the school children that some **B** scientists had **C** found meteorites that probably ca**D**me from the moon.

37. A study had **A** show that machines were **B** not any better in identifying fake back sufferers tha**C**n conventional clinical exams had **D** been.

38. The speaker had menti**A**oned to the audience of medical students tha**B**n the last 15 years had **C** seen astonishing advances i**D**n cancer research.

39. Medical experts tel**A**l that lifestyle changes and mor**B**e awareness of the cau**C**ses of cancer are beginning to h**D**ave an impact.

40. Expert ecologists agree tha**A**t poverty is the unde**B**rlying reason wh**C**y 85 percent of Madagascar's forests is been **D** destroying.

<table>
<tr><td>

11

</td><td>

Passive Voice (Simple Aspect)
Past, Present, Future Tense
Participles Used as Adjectives

</td></tr>
</table>

What Do You Know?

The Incredible Human Body

Choose the best answers to complete the quiz.

1. The human body is composed mainly of
   a) muscles
   b) water
   c) bones

2. The sense that is least developed in human beings is
   a) smell
   b) hearing
   c) taste

3. Children are cared for by
   a) pediatricians
   b) orthopedists
   c) gerontologists

4. The skin is replaced
   a) once a year
   b) every few months
   c) every few weeks

5. The central nervous system of the body is made up of
   a) the brain and nerves
   b) the heart and lungs
   c) the eyes and ears

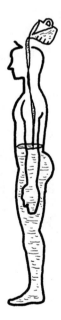

6. How many bones are found in the human body?
   a) 175
   b) 206
   c) 359

7. Blood is called
   a) the river of life
   b) the staff of life
   c) the water of life

8. More than one-third of the body's weight is composed of
   a) muscle
   b) skin
   c) bones

9. Which of these activities uses the most muscles?
   a) smiling
   b) frowning
   c) walking

10. In the body, food is processed in the
    a) skeletal system
    b) digestive system
    c) stomach

Understanding Grammar

UNDERSTAND: **Passive Voice**

Verbs belong to either the transitive or the intransitive category. Transitive verbs can have objects. They have both an active and a passive voice. Intransitive verbs cannot have objects and do not have a passive voice.

Transitive: The child broke her arm.   Her arm was broken in the fall.
              S   **V**   **O**   **S**   **V**

Intransitive: The sun set at five o'clock.
              S **V**

When the verb is transitive, there are two ways to express the information in a sentence.

a) When the **active voice** is used, the subject of the sentence is the agent (doer) of the action. The sentence also contains an object that serves as the recipient of the action. The verb is expressed in the active voice.

Active: The careless secretary destroyed the medical form.
       S   **V**   **O**
     Agent   Active form   Recipient

a heart lungs muscles bones blood					
	1	2	3	4	5

b) When the **passive voice** is used, the subject of the sentence is the recipient of the action. The doer (mentioned or understood) is the object of the sentence. The verb is expressed in the passive voice.

Passive: The medical form was destroyed. (by the secretary)
  s   **v**   **(o)**
  Recipient   Passive form   (Doer)

The passive form of the verb requires the auxiliary verb **be** + the past participle form of the main verb. The auxiliary verb **be** shows time (past, present, future).

The instructions **are written** at the bottom of the page.

That picture **was taken** last year.

Latecomers **will be left** behind.

In each example above, the form of the auxiliary verb **be** tells the time or tense of the verb phrase. The past participle form of the main verb (after **be**) tells us that the sentence is in the passive voice.

Active Voice

Present Simple	**Simple Past**	**Future Simple**
I give	I gave	I will give
you give	you gave	you will give
he gives	he gave	he will give
she gives	she gave	she will give
it gives	it gave	it will give
we give	we gave	we will give
you give	you gave	you will give
they give	they gave	they will give

Passive Voice

Present Simple	**Simple Past**	**Future Simple**
I am given	I was given	I will be given
you are given	you were given	you will be given
he is given	he was given	he will be given
she is given	she was given	she will be given
it is given	it was given	it will be given
we are given	we were given	we will be given
you are given	you were given	you will be given
they are given	they were given	they will be given

nerves a skeleton a liver a brain a skull				
6	7	8	9	10

A. Give the passive form of the verbs. Use the tense indicated in brackets.

we see (future)   **we will be seen**

1. we inspect (past)
2. they identify (future)
3. I record (present)
4. she serves (present)
5. you telephone (past)
6. he observes (future)
7. they admire (past)
8. we receive (future)
9. I exclude (past)
10. it opens (future)
11. he tells (past)
12. she refuses (past)
13. he protects (present)
14. it develops (future)
15. I follow (future)
16. you meet (present)
17. you hurt (past)
18. he marries (future)
19. we send (past)
20. he reprimands (past)

B. Change these sentences to the passive voice. **Omit the doer.**

Columbus discovered America in 1492.
America was discovered in 1492.

1. The News Network reported the story last weekend.
2. The translator translated the best-selling novel last year.
3. The doctor will examine the patient in approximately one hour.
4. The computer analyst installed the new system last year.
5. Record companies put out hundreds of new recordings every month.
6. People break their solemn promises all the time.
7. The plumber repaired the leaky faucet in just a few minutes.
8. They painted the outside of their house only last year.
9. The surgeon will remove the stitches this afternoon.
10. People speak Spanish in many countries in the world.
11. The bank will transfer the money electronically in a few hours.
12. Many farmers grow rice in countries around the world.
13. Deep sea divers located the sunken pirate ship in 1986.
14. The waiters served a delicious dinner in the dining room.
15. The team scored over one hundred goals last season.

a scar stitches/sutures gauze pads a band-aid a bandage		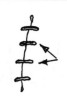	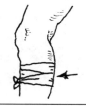	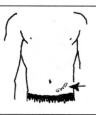	
	11	**12**	**13**	**14**	**15**

C. Change these sentences to the active voice. Use the words in brackets as the subject of the sentence.

My glasses were broken during the game. (I)
I broke my glasses during the game.

1. The papers were corrected very quickly. (that teacher)
2. My bag was inspected at the counter. (the customs officer)
3. The book will be written by next summer. (the writer)
4. A report is presented to the president every month. (the sales manager)
5. Garbage is picked up every two days. (garbage trucks)
6. Many people were treated for burns after the fire. (doctors)
7. The criminal was sentenced to life in prison. (the judge)
8. Many nurses will be laid off next year. (the hospital)
9. An unidentified flying object was sighted recently. (farmers)
10. Checks of nuclear waste sites are carried out often. (engineers)
11. The children were impressed with magic tricks. (the magician)
12. The telephone lines were knocked down. (the storm)
13. Some beautiful pictures were taken of Niagara Falls. (Jane)
14. The bank was robbed yesterday morning. (two armed men)
15. The patient was brought to the ward in a wheelchair. (an orderly)

UNDERSTAND: **When to Use the Passive Voice**

The passive voice is more common in writing than in speaking. It usually suggests more formality than the active form. News reports and textbooks often contain examples of the passive voice.

Use the passive voice in the following circumstances:

a) The agent (doer) is unknown.
   My wallet was stolen yesterday. (by someone unknown)

b) The agent (doer) is not important.
   It is written there. (by some anonymous writer)

c) The agent (doer) is so clear from the context that you don't need to identify him or her.
   The mail was delivered late again. (the letter carrier)

d) The focus is on the recipient rather that the doer.
   Many people were injured.

e) The intention is to make a general statement about something.
   News reports will be broadcast hourly.

a sling a cast crutches a cane a wheelchair				
16	**17**	**18**	**19**	**20**

A. Identify the recipient of the action in the following sentences.

<u>The hockey game</u> was lost in the third period.

1. The application form was mailed more than a week ago.
2. An ambulance rushed the injured man to the hospital.
3. Many buildings were rebuilt after the earthquake.
4. Both tea and coffee were served at the meeting.
5. A discarded cigarette started the forest fire.
6. Smoke detectors will be installed in the building.
7. The patient's pulse was taken in the emergency room.
8. The police persuaded the suspect to confess to the crime.
9. The speech will be broadcast on radio and television.
10. The accident was reported immediately after it happened.
11. The witness was interviewed by all the major networks.
12. That news magazine publishes a lot of unusual stories.
13. The athlete made a public announcement about his retirement.
14. Volunteers provided first aid to the earthquake victims.
15. The president visited the scene of the disaster.

B. Choose the sentence that is correct. Indicate whether the sentence is in the active or passive voice. Write **A** for active, or **P** for passive.

1. a) The pill took by the patient.
   b) The pill was taken by the patient.

2. a) Researchers found new cures for several diseases.
   b) Researchers were found new cures for several diseases.

3. a) The whole city destroyed by the earthquake.
   b) The whole city was destroyed by the earthquake.

4. a) The medical forms photocopied by the secretary.
   b) The medical forms were photocopied by the secretary.

5. a) Many pyramids built by the Egyptians.
   b) Many pyramids were built by the Egyptians.

6. a) The scientists finally discovered the vaccine.
   b) The scientists finally was discovered the vaccine.

an emergency room pulse a pill a capsule a tablet				
21	**22**	**23**	**24**	**25**

7. a) The news report broadcast on the morning program.

   b) The news report was broadcast on the morning program.

8. a) The police finally arrested the robber.

   b) The police finally were arrested the robber.

9. a) The X-ray taken by the radiologist.

   b) The X-ray was taken by the radiologist.

10. a) The famous architect designed a new library.

    b) The famous architect was designed a new library.

11. a) The surgical team performed brilliantly.

    b) The surgical team was performed brilliantly.

12. a) Somebody's wallet stole during the game.

    b) Somebody's wallet was stolen during the game.

13. a) The auto race won by a fraction of a second.

    b) The auto race was won by a fraction of a second.

14. a) The photograph took just before dawn.

    b) The photograph was taken just before dawn.

15. a) The telephone answered on the third or fourth ring.

    b) The telephone was answered on the third or fourth ring.

UNDERSTAND: **The Passive Voice with "By"**

In passive sentences, the agent (doer) is often omitted. However, in some circumstances the agent (doer) is mentioned using the preposition **by**.

America was discovered in 1492 by Columbus.

Use **by** to mention the doer in the following circumstances.

a) It is important to know who is responsible for the action.
   The speech was made by the president.

b) The doer is a famous person.
   The telephone was invented in Nova Scotia by Alexander Graham Bell.

c) The identity of the doer is different from what you expect.
   That painting was done by a child.

a blood pressure cuff a stethoscope an X-ray a thermometer a syringe					
	26	27	28	29	30

134

A. Decide whether it is appropriate to use **by** to identify the doer. Put a check (✔) if it is appropriate. Cross out what is not necessary.

1. That sweater was made of cashmere by a manufacturer.
2. English is taught all over the world by EFL teachers.
3. The crime was committed by a well-known lawyer.
4. Vegetables are grown in fields by farmers.
5. Research to find cures for diseases is done by researchers everywhere.
6. *Hamlet* was written in the sixteenth century by Shakespeare.
7. Tennis is practised by players throughout the world.
8. This poem was written by a poet in the 1920s.
9. Those words were spoken by President Kennedy in 1961.
10. The evening news was read by the regular newscaster.
11. Those eggs were laid by chickens in the hen house.
12. The mystery was finally solved by Sherlock Holmes.
13. Students were asked to raise their hands by the teacher.
14. That song was composed by John Lennon in 1975.
15. Our dinner was served on a platter by a waiter.

UNDERSTAND: **Present and Past Participles Used as Adjectives**

Adjectives are a common form of modifier before a noun. One form of adjective is the present or past participle. Look at the examples of adjective use below.

Jules was a **good** student.
Jim was an **interesting** student.
Jane was an **interested** student.

a stretcher
an orderly
a nurse
a doctor/ physician
a patient

31 32 33 34 35

Use the present participle (**interesting**) to give the idea that the agent (doer) caused the action. For example, Jim caused people to feel interest. Therefore, he was an **interesting** student.

Use the past participle (**interested**) to give the idea that the recipient caused the action. For example, someone (doer) caused Jane (recipient) to feel interest. Therefore, she was an **interested** student.

A. Choose the correct form of the participle.

1. The audience enjoyed the play very much. They thought it was a very (interesting / interested) production.
2. That surgeon always tries to tell everyone what to do. He is really a (dominating / dominated) kind of person.
3. The kitten could not be coaxed out of the box. It was (frightening / frightened).
4. We had a delicious dinner at the restaurant. Everyone said that it was a very (satisfying / satisfied) meal.
5. The teacher's explanation was rather unclear. Some people said it was a (confusing / confused) lesson.
6. The exam was so difficult that a number of students failed. We were depressed by the (disappointing / disappointed) results.
7. The report of the earthquake made people feel sad. It was rather (depressing / depressed) news.
8. Several people who had been invited to the dinner party showed up late. It was an (embarrassing / embarrassed) thing to happen.
9. When Mike and Julie suddenly announced their engagement, they faced a (surprising / surprised) group of friends.
10. There was a noisy construction site nearby. We were often bothered by (irritating / irritated) noises.

B. Complete the sentences with the correct participle from the following list.

amazing worried puzzling irritated boring insulted excited amusing disgusted shocking

1. The mystery of the Bermuda Triangle is still a _____ affair for many people.
2. The child had not been sleeping well and was _____ by everything.
3. The winners of the contest were so _____ that they invited everyone to celebrate.
4. The _____ news of the explosion caused pain to nearly everyone who heard about it.
5. The clown at the circus was so _____ that the children couldn't stop laughing.

a pediatrician
a dentist
a surgeon
an ophthalmologist
a psychiatrist

36   37   38   39   40

136

6. The movie was so _____ that most people left before it was even half over.

7. The streets of the city they visited were so dirty that most people were _____ by what they saw.

8. The _____ guest could not forgive the host's rude behaviour and ran out of the house.

9. The painter is also an _____ storyteller who fascinates his listeners with his incredible tales.

10. The parents were so _____ about their missing child that they called the police.

Vocabulary Challenge

Here's To Your Health

Put the missing words from each sentence on page 137 into the puzzle. Then find the hidden words.

1. A _____ is used to take a patient's temperature.
2. _____ is often taken to check for infection.
3. An _____ was taken when the woman said she thought her arm was broken.
4. A _____ is used to listen to a patient's heartbeat.
5. The lengthy operation was performed by a _____ at the hospital.
6. _____ were recommended for the boy with a sprained ankle.
7. His _____ were severely damaged after 20 years of smoking.
8. The patient was taken to the operating room by an _____.
9. Two _____ were broken in the man's leg after he fell when skiing.
10. A _____ was applied to the cut after it was stitched.
11. The elderly man was diagnosed as having had a _____ attack.
12. The patient's _____ was checked daily by the nurse.
13. A _____ is used to cover a cut.
14. His head hit the window, and his _____ was fractured in the collision.
15. A _____ is generally applied for a broken bone.
16. _____ will be used to close the cut.

Ten-Minute Grammar Games

Objects and Places

Focus: Practise the passive voice.

This game is played in teams. Each team thinks of an object or a place, and writes a characteristic of that object or place using the passive voice. The characteristic should be chosen carefully, so that it does not give the answer away immediately.

Paper is used.

The other team asks questions in the passive voice, to try to guess the place or object.

Is the paper used by a secretary?
Is the paper found in a book?

The objective is to try to guess with as few clues as possible.

How Do You Do It?

Focus: Practise the passive voice.

Students prepare a report on how to do something, using the passive voice to explain the process. They can choose from one of the following topics:

1. how to operate a piece of equipment
2. how to play a game or sport
3. how to cook a particular dish
4. how to fix something
5. how to build something

Test Yourself

A. Change these sentences to the passive voice. **Omit the doer.** Use the correct tense.

1. The team leader complimented everyone for their good work.
2. The invigilator of the exams distributed the papers late.
3. The landlord will change all the windows in the building.
4. Volunteers organize activities for senior citizens at the rec centre.
5. The teacher collected the students' journals every month.
6. The technician will repair the photocopy machine tomorrow.
7. The engineers will present the plans at the next meeting.
8. Most parents expect teenagers to be home by 11:00.
9. The chamber orchestra played only two pieces of music last night.
10. The carpet cleaners clean the carpets twice a year.

B. Choose the active or passive form to complete the sentence. Use the correct verb tense.

1. The criminal _____ (arrest) last night.
2. The frightened cat _____ (rescue) by the firefighters last week.
3. The restaurant _____ (inspect) for heath regulations soon.
4. A hurricane _____ (destroy) many houses on the island last year.
5. The museum _____ (acquire) several impressionist paintings.
6. A boring teacher _____ (put) students to sleep.
7. The hockey team _____ (eliminate) from the final series last night.
8. The new president _____ (swear in) to office tomorrow.
9. A new leader _____ (elect) head of the party next week.
10. Their financial records _____ (check) by the accountant tomorrow.

C. Check (✔) sentences where it is appropriate to mention the doer with **by**. Cross out the **by** phrase where it is not appropriate.

1. The class was taught English by the teacher.
2. Many people on the island were injured by the hurricane.
3. A candidate for the job was interviewed by the interviewer.
4. The geography exam was corrected by a committee of four.
5. The Great Pyramid was built by the pharaoh Cheops.
6. The news was announced on television by the announcer.
7. The exam results will be given in class by the teacher.
8. My drawing was submitted to the art teacher on Friday by me.
9. A good idea is not always appreciated immediately by people.
10. The forest fire was put out quickly by firefighters.

D. Choose the correct form of the adjective.

1. The movie we saw last night at the cinema had an (amazing / amazed) ending.
2. Trying to find a hotel late at night was a (frustrating / frustrated) experience.
3. The (tiring / tired) tourist decided to spend the day on the beach.
4. The (motivating / motivated) student went on to graduate school after finishing a B.A.
5. Working during heat waves can be an (exhausting / exhausted) experience.
6. People cannot be hypnotized if they are not in a (relaxing / relaxed) state.
7. Being unemployed can be a (depressing / depressed) experience for most people.
8. Swimming in cold water can produce an (exhilarating / exhilarated) experience.
9. The (discriminating / discriminated) person will not buy shoddy goods.
10. People often have (discouraging / discouraged) experiences when they are looking for work.

Score for Test Yourself: _____
40

Vocabulary Answers

1. bones	15. gauze pads	29. a syringe
2. muscles	16. crutches	30. a blood pressure cuff
3. blood	17. a wheelchair	31. an orderly
4. a heart	18. a sling	32. a doctor/physician
5. lungs	19. a cast	33. a patient
6. a brain	20. a cane	34. a nurse
7. a skull	21. a tablet	35. a stretcher
8. a liver	22. a capsule	36. a surgeon
9. nerves	23. pulse	37. a psychiatrist
10. a skeleton	24. a pill	38. a pediatrician
11. a band-aid	25. an emergency room	39. an ophthalmologist
12. stitches/sutures	26. an X-ray	40. a dentist
13. a bandage	27. a stethoscope	
14. a scar	28. a thermometer	

Passive Voice (Other Aspects, Modals)
"Would rather"

What Do You Know?

Food Riddles

Read these riddles with a partner. Try to think of the answers together. If you need help, turn to page 154 for a list of words.

1. This small round food has been used in a variety of ways for centuries. It is eaten as a main dish in the Mediterranean, but it is probably best known as an oil. It has even been used as a medicine and to clean the body. You probably don't think of it as a fruit, but it is.

2. This sweet red fruit has been enjoyed by many throughout the ages. It was recognized by countless past civilizations where it grew wild on the ground. It did not become domesticated until the dawn of refrigerated transportation, about 100 years ago. Today this fruit is eaten raw, mashed, in ice cream, and on top of pastries.

3. This food has been craved by children and adults alike for many years, but it has only been eaten in its sweet form for the last 100 years or so. It is grown in South America, and was used as a drink until the nineteenth century. Today it is enjoyed as a treat in many forms.

4. This nut has been used for centuries in everything from hair conditioner to body lotion. It even has a shape named after it. As early as 2500 BC, this food was grown in Greece and served as a favourite dish. Today it is grown all over the world, and eaten as a snack or combined with a large variety of other foods both as a main course and as a dessert.

5. This fruit is being used by health-conscious people everywhere. It is valued for its energy boost and low calories. The pink variety of this fruit is full of vitamins. The white variety tastes nearly as juicy and sweet. It is a cross between two other fruits, and comes originally from a tropical island.

141

Understanding Grammar

UNDERSTAND: **Passive Voice (Other Aspects)**

The passive voice can be used in the following cases:

    a) sentences that express continuous action
    b) sentences that express perfective aspect
    c) sentences that express future time with **be going to**

UNDERSTAND: **Passive Voice with the Continuous Aspect**

To form the passive voice with continuous action, it is necessary to use the present participle form **being** + the past participle form of the verb. Use the correct form of the verb **be** according to person (first, second, or third) and tense (past or present).

    It **is**…
    We **were**…

Use **being** to indicate continuous action + the past participle of the main verb.

    It **is being done** now.
    We **were being interviewed** then.

A. Write the verbs below in the passive form.

    is doing **is being done**

1. are exposing		11. is damaging
2. was watching		12. are painting
3. is controlling		13. were studying
4. are manufacturing		14. is writing
5. is producing		15. was examining
6. was planning		16. was employing
7. were discovering		17. are discriminating
8. am sending		18. was reviewing
9. is forgetting		19. were improving
10. were remembering		20. am helping

almonds walnuts pecans peanuts cashews	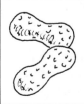			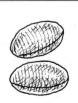	
	1	2	3	4	5

B. Write the following sentences in the passive voice. Omit mention of the agent (doer) of the action.

Scientists are doing research in Chicago.
Research is being done in Chicago.

1. The committee is interviewing the candidate now.
2. Detectives are interrogating the burglary suspect.
3. The owners are remodelling our favourite restaurant.
4. A mechanic is repairing their old car.
5. The business partners are signing the contract.
6. The dressmaker is shortening my new party dress.
7. Painters are painting the front door.
8. Someone is helping my neighbour already.
9. Robbers are holding up the bank.
10. The contractors are still building the house.

C. Write the sentences in the active voice. Use the words in brackets as the subject of the sentence.

The politician was being investigated for corruption. (a judge)
A judge was investigating the politician for corruption.

1. The New Year's party was being organized. (the social committee)
2. The walnuts and pecans were being chopped. (the kitchen staff)
3. The swimmer was being given mouth-to-mouth resuscitation. (the lifeguard)
4. The athletes were being tested for drug use. (the team doctor)
5. The elderly woman was being cared for. (a nurse)
6. The firefighter was being treated for burns. (burn specialists)
7. Cooks were being asked to do too much overtime. (the restaurant)
8. The hotel rooms were being cleaned. (housekeepers)
9. The fax was being sent in the other office. (the secretary)
10. The math class was being kept in after school. (the teacher)

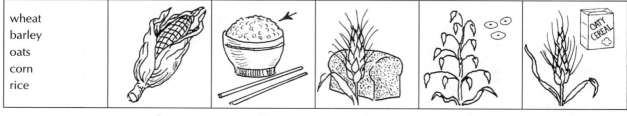

wheat barley oats corn rice				
6	7	8	9	10

UNDERSTAND: **Passive Voice with the Perfective Aspect**

To form the passive voice with perfective aspect, use the auxiliary verb **have** + **been** + the past participle form of the main verb. The auxiliary **have** can indicate past, present, or future time.

> The secretarial position **has been filled**.
> The contract **had been signed** by the time I arrived.
> The job **will have been advertised** in the weekend newspaper.

> **TEACHER'S BOX:** The perfective aspect is not used with the continuous form in the passive voice. Students may confuse **been** and **being** when they form the verb phrase with **have been** + the main verb.

A. Change the simple passive form to the present perfect passive form.

It was sent yesterday.   **It has been sent.**

1. It was done before.
2. They were selected for the job.
3. It was translated into many languages.
4. It was hidden from sight.
5. We were criticized for it.
6. They were shown many samples.
7. She was told that she was right.
8. It was noticed by several people.
9. It was broken.
10. It was tried before.

B. Write these sentences in the past perfect passive form. **Omit mention of the agent (doer).**

The cleaners had washed all the windows.

All the windows had been washed.

1. The ambassador had consulted many foreign leaders.
2. The manager had written the report before the due date.
3. The janitor had not fixed the sink before we moved in.
4. That association had provided many meals for homeless people.
5. The protesters had circulated a petition against the project.
6. The airline had announced our flight twice before we heard it.
7. News of the terrible accident had shocked everyone.
8. The researchers had conducted many different experiments.
9. The new restaurant had hired at least 50 new employees.
10. The college had announced the exam schedules for the fall term.

parsley garlic tuna a lobster salmon					
	11	12	13	14	15

C. Complete the sentences with the verbs below. Use the present perfect or past perfect passive form of the verbs.

That course **has been taught** (teach) here for years.

resolve   send   fill in   fascinate   postpone   wash   edit   hold   read over   fill

1. The grapes _____ before the hungry children started to eat them.
2. The conflict _____. You don't need to worry about it anymore.
3. The author's manuscript _____ by a friend before it was sent to the publisher.
4. The game _____ because of the thunder showers that meteorologists are predicting.
5. The package of documents we needed _____ by special delivery the day before.
6. People _____ for ages by the possibility that alien beings exist in outer space.
7. All the forms _____ by the time the registration desk closed.
8. An annual convention _____ in a different country each year since the association was formed.
9. All the positions that were advertised _____ by the time I applied.
10. My history assignment didn't have any spelling errors because it _____ carefully beforehand.

UNDERSTAND: **Passive Voice and Future Time with "Be going to"**

To form the passive voice with **be going to** (for future time), use **be going to** + the base form of **be** + past participle.

The book **is going to be sold** in the book store.

A. Put the verb phrase in the passive form with "be going to."
1. The heating in our building _____ (turn off) on the weekend.
2. The new concert hall _____ (open) some time early next year.
3. The catalogue _____ (mail) to all our former customers next week.
4. The results of the final exams _____ (post) on the bulletin board near the office.
5. My cousin and her fiancé _____ (marry) in the cathedral downtown.
6. The barley and oats _____ (grind) into flour.
7. All the new cereals _____ (sample) before we ship them out to customers.
8. The zucchini and eggplant _____ (pack) for shipping immediately.
9. All the children in the class _____ (invite) to the birthday party on Saturday.
10. The difficult grammar _____ (include) in the final exam.

squash pumpkin eggplant zucchini asparagus					
	16	17	18	19	20

B. Look at the pictures and write a passive sentence with **be going to** describing what is probably going to happen next. Use the verbs under the pictures.

Catch

Arrest

Bite

Tow

Turn off

Collect

Wash

Serve

Blow out

TEACHER'S BOX: Another way of expressing **be going to** + past participle is the phrase **"about to be"** + past participle: "The car is going to be towed away." "The car is about to be towed away." The phrase **about to be** suggests immediacy.

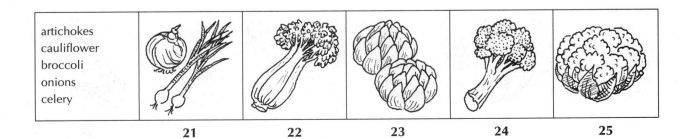

artichokes				
cauliflower				
broccoli				
onions				
celery				
	21	22	23	24	25

UNDERSTAND: **"Would rather"**

Use **would rather** to express a preference in response to a question.

> Would you like an apple or a pear?
>
> I **would rather** have a pear.

When comparing two things, use **would rather** + verb + **than** to express a preference. The contraction of **would rather** is the subject pronoun + **'d rather**.

> I would rather eat than sleep.
>
> **I'd rather** eat than sleep.

"Would rather" When the Subject Does Not Change

When the subject is the same in both parts of a comparison, use **would rather** + the base form of the verb. The negative form is **would rather not** + the base form of the verb.

> I **would rather** learn French than play basketball.   I **would rather not eat** that.

A. Make sentences comparing two activities with **I'd rather...than**. Use the activity in bold type as your preference.

go bowling/**go skating**

I'd rather go skating than go bowling.

1. **go to the film festival**/go to a baseball game
2. **stay home**/go out this evening
3. have a fruit juice/**have a soft drink**
4. **take a plane**/take a train
5. play computer games/**read a book**
6. **go to the beach**/go on a tour
7. **sleep late on weekends**/get up early on weekends
8. be rich and unhappy/**be poor and happy**
9. cook dinner myself/**order take-out food**
10. **eat artichokes**/eat broccoli

B. Complete the sentences with your own ideas.

1. I would rather do more homework than _____ .
2. Sports teams would rather _____ than lose a game.
3. Most people would rather sleep in than _____ .

spinach pepper radishes lettuce peas				
	26	27	28	29	30

4. Some people would rather _____ than work.

5. I would rather _____ than eat meat.

6. We would rather be happy than be _____ .

7. My friend would rather be late than _____ .

8. Most people would rather _____ than be poor.

9. I would rather speak _____ than speak _____ .

10. I would rather be on time than _____ .

"Would rather" When the Subject Changes

When the preference involves having someone else do something, and two different subjects are identified, use **would rather** + the subject + the past tense form of the verb.

> Will Bob carry your suitcase?
>
> I would rather **you carried it**.

The negative form of **would rather** in this case is **would rather** + subject + **did not** + base form of the verb.

> Do you mind if I tell Jill about this?
>
> I'd **rather** you **didn't tell** anyone.

A. Choose the best verb to complete the sentence. Put it in the correct tense.

come   not put   cook   cancel   write   not give   send   take   not find out   consult

1. I would rather someone else _____ this article.

2. She would rather her husband _____ dinner this evening.

3. We would rather they _____ us before deciding on the date.

4. Jun would rather his brother _____ sugar in the lemonade.

5. Suzanna would rather we _____ to dinner on any other night.

6. His father would rather Jim _____ driving lessons at school.

7. The class would rather the teacher _____ homework today.

8. The kids would rather their mother _____ who ate the cookies.

9. The team would rather the coach _____ the game if it rains.

10. Hiroshi would rather his parents _____ him to study abroad.

a coconut
a watermelon
a grapefruit
a lime
a lemon

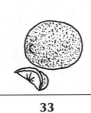

| 31 | 32 | 33 | 34 | 35 |

B. Read the short conversations and fill in the blanks with the verb in the present or past tense.

1. Do you want to contact all the guests to tell them about the change in plans?
   No, I'd rather you (call) _____ them.

2. Shall I call the painter this weekend?
   No, I'd rather (do) _____ it myself.

3. Do you mind if I smoke in this room?
   I would rather you (not smoke) _____ anywhere in the house.

4. Would you like to go sightseeing with us tomorrow?
   I'd rather (go) _____ by myself.

5. Shall I call the plumber to fix the leak?
   Yes. I'd rather you (not try) _____ to fix it yourself.

6. Shall I tell everyone the good news now?
   I would rather you (wait) _____ a few more days.

7. Is it all right if people bring friends to the party?
   I'd rather everyone (come) _____ alone.

8. Would you like to meet at the coffee shop after class?
   I'm really tired. I'd rather (go) _____ straight home.

9. Do you want some of the students to begin working on the project?
   I'd rather they (not start) _____ until everyone is ready.

10. Do you want me to buy a new TV for the extra room?
    I'd rather you (not spend) _____ any more money for a while.

a fruit salad grapes strawberries blueberries a cantaloupe					
	36	37	38	39	40

Vocabulary Challenge

The Food Puzzle

Use the clues to complete the puzzle.

Across

3. _____ are often used in breakfast cereal, as well as in breads or muffins.

5. A large _____ is usually cut in slices and served at the mid-summer picnic.

7. The juicy red and green _____ were arranged in a fruit bowl on the dining-room table.

8. _____ is often mixed with mayonnaise and spread on bread to make a sandwich.

9. A _____ was chosen by the restaurant guest, and then cooked for dinner.

11. The crisp green _____ was chopped and prepared for cooking.

12. The large white _____ was cut into pieces and added to the soup.

14. _____ are often ground and made into a spread for sandwiches.

15. The chef's eyes began to water as she sliced the pungent _____ .

18. The juicy orange _____ was cut into chunks and added to the fruit salad.

20. The large pink _____ was squeezed and made into juice.

Down

1. _____ have to be chopped before they can be used in muffins or cake.

2. The juicy red _____ were picked and put into baskets to go to market.

4. The small green _____ were cooked and made into a thick soup.

5. The _____ was ground into flour, to be used in bread.

6. The _____ was sliced and put on the table next to the tea pot.

7. The _____ was chopped and added to the spaghetti sauce.

10. The _____ was sliced and served on a fish platter as the main course for dinner.

13. The large orange _____ was carved and set out on the doorstep for Halloween.

16. The _____ was washed and cooked as a side dish, next to the meat and potatoes.

17. The flaked white _____ was chopped and added to the cookies.

19. Several red and green _____ were sliced and put on the pizza.

Ten-Minute Grammar Games

Tell Me the Future

Focus: Practise expressing future time with the passive voice.

Students work in groups to predict what the world will be like 20 years from now. They brainstorm ideas, and write sentences for each of the categories listed below, using the passive voice.

In the future, many jobs will be done by robots.
Small telephones are going to be carried by everyone.

Jobs

Communication

Food

Child care

Medicine

Travel

The family unit

Education

Leisure time

Technology

Find Someone

Focus: Practise using **would rather**.

The aim is for students to find at least one person who fits each description on the list. Students walk around the room asking each other questions. When a person answers "Yes," his or her name is written beside the description on the list. The first person to finish is the winner. Students in the class can be asked to confirm or deny the information as the winner reads it out.

Find someone who would rather…

1. go sailing than do any other water sport
2. cook than eat in a restaurant
3. listen to the radio than watch TV
4. get up early on the weekend than sleep in
5. have a cat than have a dog
6. give a party than attend one
7. write a letter than make a long-distance phone call
8. work than go to school full-time
9. read non-fiction than read a novel
10. go to a movie theatre than watch a video
11. eat a big breakfast than eat a big dinner
12. wear blue jeans than wear designer clothes

Test Yourself

A. Find the errors in the verb phrases in bold type and correct them. Check (✔) correct sentences.

1. Many workers were injured while that bridge **was be built**.
2. The old theatre downtown **is** currently **being renovate**.
3. The interviews **are been conducted** at this very moment.
4. Some tourists **are being show** around the ruins.
5. Francisco **is being hired for** the position in accounting.
6. The old manuscripts **are been kept** in the Rare Book Room.
7. The suspect **is being question** by the police officers.
8. Anne and May **are being interviewed** for the job.
9. The bridge **is being repair** by a construction crew.
10. Hiroshi **is been given** a tour of the city by his friends.

B. Put the following sentences in the passive form. Omit the doer if it is not necessary.

He has made all the preparations for the party.
All the preparations for the party have been made.

1. The social committee has prepared a huge celebration for the anniversary.
2. The eruption of the volcano has caused a great deal of destruction.
3. People have kept those manuscripts under lock and key for centuries.

4. Borrowers have repaid very little of the money that was borrowed.
5. The composer Schubert had only finished part of the symphony when he died.
6. Volunteers had already cleaned up most of the damage by the time we arrived.
7. Fire had completely destroyed the building by the time the fire department got there.
8. A colony of ants had overrun the picnic by the time we finished eating.
9. The box office had sold all the tickets for the play by the time we arrived at the theatre.
10. The rampaging river has flooded large sections of the downtown area.

C. Choose the best verb to complete each sentence. Use the passive voice with **be going to**.

The date of the exam **is going to be announced** soon.

tow   sell   hold up   correct   give   teach   put   invite   take   meet

1. All the merchandise _____ by the weekend.
2. The children _____ to bed early tonight.
3. We hope that the exams _____ soon.
4. Illegally parked cars _____ by the city.
5. Everyone in the class _____ to the party.
6. The tourists _____ to see a play at the theatre.
7. Mei Ling's course _____ in English.
8. Traffic _____ because of the accident.
9. Pablo's sister _____ at the airport by the whole family.
10. Ginette _____ the results of her audition today.

D. Fill in the blanks with the correct form of the verb in brackets.

1. Would you like to play volleyball?
   I'd rather _____ (play) badminton.

2. Should I decide on next week's schedule now?
   I'd rather you _____ (wait) until tomorrow.

3. Shall I buy a new car or a used one?
   I'd rather you _____ (not buy) a car at all.

4. Do you want to go to the gym this afternoon?
   It's a beautiful day; we'd rather _____ (spend) the day outdoors.

5. Do you like to write to your friends or talk on the phone?
   I don't like either. I'd rather _____ (speak) to them in person.

6. Do the employees like working on weekends?
   Of course not. They would rather _____ (put in) extra hours during the week.

7. Do you want to travel to China or Thailand on your next holiday?
   I'd rather _____ (visit) Thailand than China this year.

8. Would you prefer tea of coffee after dinner?
   I'd rather _____ (have) coffee tonight.

9. Shall I tell them to deliver the bed next week?

   I'd rather you _____ (tell) them to deliver it as soon as possible.

10. Do you mind if they wait outside the office?

    I'd rather they _____ (come back) in one hour.

    Score for Test Yourself: _____
    40

Vocabulary for page 141

chocolate   grapefruit   almonds   strawberries   olives

Vocabulary Answers

1. peanuts	15. garlic	29. lettuce
2. cashews	16. pumpkin	30. radishes
3. almonds	17. eggplant	31. a watermelon
4. pecans	18. asparagus	32. a lemon
5. walnuts	19. squash	33. a lime
6. corn	20. zucchini	34. a coconut
7. rice	21. onions	35. a grapefruit
8. wheat	22. celery	36. a cantaloupe
9. oats	23. artichokes	37. strawberries
10. barley	24. broccoli	38. a fruit salad
11. tuna	25. cauliflower	39. blueberries
12. a lobster	26. pepper	40. grapes
13. salmon	27. peas	
14. parsley	28. spinach	

What Do You Know?

Who Could Do It For Me?

Check off the things you hate to do. Then think about who you would like to do them instead, and write your idea in brackets.

do housework (a robot)

1. answer the phone when I'm working
2. feed the cat in the morning
3. do the dishes after supper
4. cut the grass on the weekend
5. wash my car thoroughly
6. make a speech in public
7. do my homework
8. take out the garbage
9. pay household bills
10. prepare food for a party
11. cook my own dinner
12. paint the house
13. do my income taxes
14. clean the garage
15. sew fancy clothes
16. walk the dog at night
17. go grocery shopping
18. write exams
19. clean my oven
20. write thank-you notes

Understanding Grammar

UNDERSTAND: **Causative Statements with "Have"**

In a causative statement, the verb **have** indicates that two people (a causer and a doer) are responsible for the action described in the statement. The causer either can't or doesn't want to do the action and therefore causes someone else to do it.

> Marla **has the secretary** open the mail.

Causative Statements When Both Causer and Doer Are Mentioned

A causative relationship can be expressed when both the causer and the doer are mentioned in the sentence.

> Marla has her secretary open the mail.
> Causer   Doer Action

When both the causer and the doer are mentioned in a causative statement, the causative verb **have** can be in any form (past, future, continuous , etc.). The main verb is expressed in the base form.

> Marla will have her secretary open the mail.
> Causer + **have** + doer + base form of the main verb

A. Identify the causer and the doer in the sentences below. Underline the causer and circle the doer.

Franco is having the (veterinarian) examine his dog.

1. The driver will have the mechanic change the tire before the next trip.
2. The lawyer had her assistant look in the filing cabinet for the missing documents.
3. The children's parents had the dentist check the children's teeth every six months.
4. The cadet had the military barber cut his hair as short as possible.
5. The exhausted tourist had the waiter from room service bring him breakfast in bed.
6. The homeroom teacher has the students clean their desks thoroughly every week.
7. Mrs. Williams had her son take the empty bottles to the recycling bin.
8. The priest had the bride and groom repeat their wedding vows after him.
9. Fred Burns has the coffee shop send coffee and donuts to his office every morning.
10. Mr. Tanaka had room service pick up his laundry for dry cleaning.

an orthodontist a physiotherapist a pharmacist a veterinarian an ophthalmologist					
	1	2	3	4	5

B. Complete the sentences by choosing a doer from the list below.

> **my brothers   the students   the players   patients   the actors   the company
> the criminal   a hairdresser   a cleaning service   the landlord**

1. Most of the employees are having _____ deposit their pay directly in their bank accounts.
2. The coach had _____ change their tactics in the last football game.
3. Nancy usually has _____ wash the walls in her apartment once a year.
4. A physiotherapist generally has _____ continue their exercises on their own at home.
5. My mother usually had _____ wash the dinner dishes when we had had guests.
6. The tenant had _____ repair the leak in the roof before it got worse.
7. The new teacher will have _____ hand in their homework before class.
8. The police officer had _____ put his hands on the police car.
9. The director had _____ rehearse the play for weeks before the performance.
10. Mrs. Greene is having _____ cut and style her hair for the party.

Causative Statements When Only the Causer Is Mentioned

A causative relationship can be expressed when only the causer is mentioned.

> May had her speech written for her.
> Causer   Object   Action

The grammatical form of the sentence indicates that the action was caused by one person and done by another person. The causative verb can be expressed in any tense. The main verb is expressed in the past participle form.

> Marla will have her speech translated.
> Causer   + **have**   + object + past participle of the main verb

A. Rewrite the sentences omitting mention of the doer and making necessary changes.

> Marla will have Frank translate her speech.
> **Marla will have her speech translated.**

1. The Johnsons are having someone redecorate their house.
2. Mario has the doctor check his blood pressure every week.
3. Professor Jones will have someone proofread his manuscript before he sends it to the publisher.

a solicitor a barrister a judge an accountant an architect		TAX SERVICE		
	6	7	8	9	10

158

4. The famous actress had an artist paint her portrait.
5. The manufacturer has an inspector check the cars before they leave the factory.
6. Michael Grey had a tailor shorten his new pants.
7. My neighbours are having someone replace their old windows.
8. Francine is having a mechanic repair her car this week.
9. Susy had a neighbour look after her cat while she was away.
10. Jackson had room service bring his dinner to his room.

UNDERSTAND: **Causative Statements with "Get"**

In a causative statement, the verb **have** can be replaced with the verb **get** with a small difference in form. With **get**, the main verb is expressed as the infinitive.

Marla will get her secretary to open the mail.
Causer   + **get**   + doer   + infinitive form of the main verb

A. Make causative statements using these elements and **got** (past tense).

make the bed/mother/lazy son
The mother got her lazy son to make the bed.

1. Janet/her sister/lend her a sweater
2. the players/train harder/the coach
3. do the shopping/the wife/the husband
4. teacher/erase the board/a student
5. the telephone company/pay the bill/the deadbeat
6. Paula/marry her/her boyfriend Fred
7. wash the dishes/Gaby/her roommate
8. my friend/type her essay/me
9. smile/the clown/the children
10. practise the piano/her students/the music teacher

TEACHER'S BOX: The choice of **got** as the causative verb implies that more effort was required to cause the action to take place: "Anne had Jim pass her the paper." (It was easier for Jim to reach the paper.) but, "Mr. Jones got his son to cut the grass." (His son had to be persuaded.) When the doer is omitted in a causative statement, there is no difference in the form of **get** and **had**: "She had the windows washed." or "She got the windows washed."

a jeweller
an editor
a locksmith
a janitor
a barber

11   12   13   14   15

B. Choose the person who was probably the doer in these sentences.

She had her hair cut.

✔ a) a hairdresser
   b) a mechanic
   c) her cat

1. They had their tires changed.
   a) the police
   b) a mechanic
   c) a driver

2. The lawyer had the fine reduced.
   a) the police
   b) the client
   c) the judge

3. She had the flowers planted.
   a) the gardener
   b) the janitor
   c) the neighbour

4. They had the house designed.
   a) a painter
   b) a builder
   c) an architect

5. She had her will made.
   a) a friend
   b) a lawyer
   c) an umpire

6. He had his teeth examined.
   a) a pharmacist
   b) a pediatrician
   c) an orthodontist

7. She had her pet vaccinated.
   a) the doctor
   b) the barber
   c) the vet

8. We had our kitchen sink fixed.
   a) a plumber
   b) a jeweller
   c) a lifeguard

9. You had the furniture repaired.
   a) a caterer
   b) an electrician
   c) a carpenter

10. They had a car key made.
   a) a mechanic
   b) a locksmith
   c) a bus driver

an usher an umpire a coach a lifeguard a caterer					
	16	17	18	19	20

C. Go back to the previous exercise and use the information to write causative sentences with **got**. Use a separate sheet of paper.

She got the hairdresser to cut her hair.

UNDERSTAND: **Use of the Verb "Make"**

To give the meaning of producing or constructing something concrete, use the verb **make**. Although **make** and **do** have similar meanings, it is not possible to use **do** in the categories of activity below.

a) make clothes
b) make furniture
c) make three dimensional art and film
d) make manufactured products
e) make food (meals)

A. Match each of the following actions to a category above.

make spaghetti   **e**

1. make a salad
2. make plastic containers
3. make a sculpture
4. make a movie
5. make soup
6. make cars
7. make shoes
8. make a cake
9. make a shirt
10. make toys

11. make a statue
12. make a sauce
13. make a delicious meal
14. make a gown
15. make a desk
16. make breakfast
17. make a scarf
18. make a tool
19. make a coffee table
20. make appetizers

a window washer a carpenter an orderly a florist a baby-sitter					
	21	22	23	24	25

UNDERSTAND: **"Make" and "Do"**

Make and **do** are used to describe an activity, action, or task. The basic meaning of the verbs **make** and **do** is the same, but each of them combines with particular words and expressions that must be learned by heart.

Make	**Do**
make a mistake	do the dishes
make a speech	do the shopping
make a phone call	do your homework
make an effort	do work
make a decision	do a good job
make love	do the laundry
make war	do the cooking
make noise	do exercise
make an excuse	do well in something
make plans	do badly in something
make reservations	do a favour
make your bed	do your duty
make money	do research
make time	do an assignment
make friends	do your best
make enemies	do a dance
make sense	do yoga
make a deal	do tricks
make a suggestion	do damage
make up your mind	do good
make it better	do harm
make it worse	
make a big deal of it	
make someone happy	
make someone sad	
make a fuss	
make a fool of yourself	
make a nuisance of yourself	

a bricklayer
a butcher
a seamstress
a decorator
an esthetician

A. Complete the sentences with **make** or **do**. Put the verb in the correct tense.

1. She _____ yoga for the past three months and is finally learning to relax.

2. Some people are not good at _____ up their minds about things.

3. The hockey player _____ special exercises for his back since his last accident.

4. The suggestion she _____ turned out to be the best we had ever received.

5. That student arrives late every day and always _____ a different excuse.

6. Many scientists _____ research now to find cures for different illnesses.

7. Car manufacturers _____ a lot of money these days, selling smaller cars.

8. The organizers _____ such a good job at the last party that they were paid a bonus.

9. The politician _____ a very stirring speech during the last election campaign.

10. Most children don't _____ homework regularly unless they are supervised.

11. Bad eating habits and lack of exercise can _____ serious harm to your health.

12. Last year we _____ reservations too late and couldn't get the hotel we wanted.

13. The graduating students _____ many assignments so far this semester.

14. Anne and Gaston _____ many new friends since they arrived in Vancouver.

15. Their mother was really angry because they hadn't _____ the dishes when she got home.

Vocabulary Challenge

Jobs and Professions

Complete the puzzle, using the clues below. Then find the hidden message.

1. The judge had the _____ rephrase her argument for the jury.

2. The young couple got the _____ to cut thick juicy steaks for their barbecue.

3. The latecomers had the _____ show them to their seats after the show had begun.

4. I had the _____ fill my prescription after my visit to the doctor.

5. The _____ made the patient read the eye chart three times before he decided on a prescription.

6. The swimmer made the _____ dive in after her when he heard her screams.

7. The city planners had an _____ design the new wing for the museum.

8. The young woman had the _____ apply her make-up before her wedding.

9. The _____ made the team do 50 push-ups a day to get in shape for the game.

10. The _____ had the reporter check the source of his quotes before agreeing to print them in the newspaper.

11. The architect had the _____ build a new wall on the house he was renovating.

12. The hospital patient had the _____ wheel him to the sun room at the end of the corridor.

13. The bride had the _____ design a bouquet of roses and lilies for her wedding bouquet.

14. The building manager had the _____ clean all of the windows in the skyscraper.

15. The _____ made the disorganized client find all his tax receipts before she would do his taxes.

16. The _____ made the dog lie down so that he could examine its leg.

17. The frightened couple got the _____ to change all the locks in their house after the robbery.

Ten Minute Grammar Games

Quick Draw

Focus: Practise using **make** and **do**.

Students work in teams. A student selects one of the actions listed below and draws the action on the board. The other students in the team are given a time limit of 20 seconds to guess what the action is. If the team guesses within the time limit, it gets a point.

Teams take turns drawing the ideas, and guessing. The team with the most points wins.

make a mistake	do the dishes
make a speech	do the shopping
make a phone call	do your homework
make noise	do work
make an excuse	do the laundry
make plans	do the cooking
make reservations	do exercise
make your bed	do well in something
make money	do badly in something
make friends	do a favour
make a deal	do research
make a suggestion	do an assignment
make someone happy	do a dance
make someone sad	do yoga
make a fuss	do tricks
make a fool of yourself	
make a nuisance of yourself	

Sentence Ends

Focus: Practise using **make** and **do**.

Students work in pairs to complete the sentences. The team with the most creative answers wins.

1. A good way to make more money, is to …
2. One way to apologize if you make a mistake is…
3. If I did badly in something, I would…
4. A good excuse to make for not doing your homework is…
5. To do a favour for someone, you can…
6. If you want to do well in something, you should…
7. A good way to make friends is…
8. When you have to make a speech in public, you should…
9. The best thing to do when someone makes a nuisance of himself or herself is…
10. If you want to avoid making enemies, don't…

Test Yourself

A. Complete the sentences by choosing a causer from the list below.

> **the company   the doctor   the politician   the hostess   the conductor**
> **the artist   the teacher   the customer   the editor   the tour guide**

1. _____ had the nurse take the patient's temperature.
2. _____ had the writer make a few changes in the manuscript.
3. _____ is having an interior decorator redesign their offices.
4. _____ always has his speeches written by someone else.
5. _____ had the tourists wait in the bus until the rain had stopped.
6. _____ had the musicians practise the piece of music many times.
7. _____ had the model keep exactly the same pose for several hours.
8. _____ had the bank teller bring his bank book up to date.
9. _____ had her guests help themselves to food from the buffet table.
10. _____ had the students write a composition every week.

B. Rewrite the sentences omitting mention of the doer.

1. The vacationers had the telephone company disconnect their phone while they were away.
2. The bus driver had the mechanic check the brakes before he took the vehicle on the road.
3. We had the neighbour's son paint our kitchen cupboards after we cleaned them.
4. I had my older sister check my homework over very carefully before I gave it to the teacher.
5. Margot had the florist arrange the flowers in an attractive bouquet before she left the store.
6. The young lawyer had the hairdresser cut her hair before she appeared in court.
7. The City of Montreal had the municipal workers clear the snow before the streets became dangerous.
8. My older brother had me clean the house before my parents came back from vacation.
9. The airline had the baggage handlers load the missing baggage on the next flight.
10. The animal lover had the vet vaccinate his cat to protect it from rabies.

C. Rewrite these sentences using **get** as the causative verb.

1. Janet had John change the light bulbs.
2. The mother has the children wash the dishes.
3. The director had the movie star act in his new film.
4. The old couple has the supermarket deliver their groceries.
5. The kindergarten teacher has the kids put away their toys.
6. Max had his father read him a story before he went to bed.
7. Most schools have their students recycle paper.
8. The company had all its employees take computer courses.
9. The baby-sitter had the children go to bed early.
10. Francisco had his friends help him move his furniture.

166

D. Put the following activities under **make** or **do**. Look back at the lists on page 161 only when you need help.

research   the dishes   homework   the laundry   a mistake   dinner   an effort   the bed
a deal   exercise   a cake   friends   the shopping   a favour   noise   money   enemies
a good job   sense   reservations

Make	Do

Score for Test Yourself: _____
40

Note: Allot half a point for each activity in section D.

Vocabulary Answers

1. an ophthalmologist
2. a pharmacist
3. a veterinarian
4. an orthodontist
5. a physiotherapist
6. a judge
7. an architect
8. an accountant
9. a barrister
10. a solicitor
11. a jeweller
12. a locksmith
13. a barber
14. a janitor
15. an editor
16. a lifeguard
17. a coach
18. a caterer
19. an usher
20. an umpire
21. a florist
22. a carpenter
23. a baby-sitter
24. a window washer
25. an orderly
26. a seamstress
27. a bricklayer
28. a decorator
29. an esthetician
30. a butcher

14

Question Review
Yes/no Questions
Short Answers
Negative Questions
WH-Information Questions
"Who" and "What" as Subjects in Questions

Questions with "Like," "Be like," "Look like"

What Do You Know?

Personal Portraits

Work in pairs. Take turns asking and answering the questionnaire in pairs.

1. How many meals do you eat a day?
2. How often do you go to the movies?
3. Where would you like to go on vacation?
4. Would you be afraid to go sky diving?
5. What kind of music do you like?
6. Where were you born?
7. When did you first take an airplane?
8. How do you say the name of your country in your language?
9. Do you have brothers or sisters?
10. What is your favorite colour?
11. Are you a member of any political party?
12. How many languages can you speak?
13. Could you live with a person who smoked?
14. How far away from your job do you live?
15. Will you go on vacation this year?
16. When was the last time you rode a bicycle?
17. Why are you studying English?
18. Who is the most famous person in your country?
19. How long has your country existed?
20. When did you move to your present apartment or house?

Understanding Grammar

UNDERSTAND: **Yes/No Questions**

Yes/no questions request the answer **Yes** or **No**. Yes/no questions are formed in two ways.

Inversion of Word Order

To form yes/no questions, you can invert subject and verb word order (except with the present simple or simple past tenses). Note that the form of the main verb can be the base form, the past participle, or the present participle.

With **be** and the modal auxiliary verbs, use the base form of the main verb.

> Are you happy?
> Can you swim?
> Should we park?
> Will she sing?

With the perfective aspect or the passive voice, use the past participle form of the main verb.

> Have you been to Rome?
> Had you met before?
> Was he seen by the police?
> Is it written anywhere?

With the continuous aspect, use the present participle of the main verb.

> Is it raining outside?
> Were they speaking to us?
> Have they been living there long?

A. Change these sentences to question form.

> Joseph is reading.   **Is Joseph reading?**

1. Anna can relax on the weekend.
2. François has walked around the block twice.
3. Lin would buy a new car if he had the money.
4. Poling should take a couple of computer courses.
5. We were embarrassed by all the attention.
6. The show will begin at eight o'clock sharp.
7. A poster was put up at the end of the hall.

| a high-rise |
| a balcony |
| an awning |
| a roof terrace |
| a skyscraper |

1   2   3   4   5

8. The game had started before we arrived.
9. They are studying for the TOEFL exam.
10. George Washington could speak French.
11. That movie was seen by many people.
12. Joe has been working there for a long time.
13. My friends have gone to Toronto.
14. Sue and Jun have bought a new car.
15. Max was working in a skyscraper last year.

Use of the Dummy Auxiliary "Do"

Yes/no questions can also be formed by using the auxiliary verb **do** (does) or **did** at the beginning of the question. Note that the auxiliary verb **do** (**does**) is used for present time and **did** is used for past time.

Do you live here?
Does she like it here?
Did you go to work yesterday?

A. Change these sentences to question form.

I like cheese.   **Do you like cheese?**

1. Our neighbours like to sit on their balcony every evening.
2. Our best friends live next door to us.
3. Sarah speaks five European languages.
4. Jack called Mimi from a phone booth.
5. The Dunns ride horses on the weekend.
6. There was a lot of litter in the park.
7. This billboard attracts a lot of attention.
8. Maxine left the front door unlocked.
9. Revolving doors help conserve energy in buildings.
10. The subway stops running at 11:00.
11. The children crossed the street at the crosswalk.
12. We saw a lot of neon signs in the city.
13. Milo said that he liked opera.
14. Mike swims before breakfast every day.
15. Ambulances and police cars both have sirens.

a fire hydrant a phone booth a parking meter a parking lot a courier					
	6	7	8	9	10

UNDERSTAND: **Short Answers**

To respond to yes/no questions, the short answer form is generally used. Use **yes** or **no** + subject + auxiliary verb. With negative short answers, use contractions.

Is this your book?	Yes, it is.
Do you like music?	Yes, I do.
Have you been to Rome?	No, I haven't.

A. Complete the answers to the questions with short answer form.

1. Has that woman ever broken the law?

   _____ . She isn't a person who commits illegal acts.

2. Were they disappointed when they lost the final game?

   _____ , but they are getting over it now.

3. Will the dancers tour North America?

   _____ . Only European tours have been planned.

4. Can you write with your left hand?

   _____ , but I wish I could.

5. Do you know how to interpret sign language?

   _____ . My sister is mute.

6. Have they ever travelled by ship?

   _____ . They say it's too expensive and takes too long.

7. Did you meet any interesting people while you were travelling?

   _____ . I met someone who spoke 13 languages.

8. Was she chosen to represent her school in the debate?

   _____ . Her classmate was chosen to debate.

9. Is he still working as hard as he used to?

   _____ . He will never change.

10. Have you been studying the martial arts for long?

    _____ . I only began two months ago.

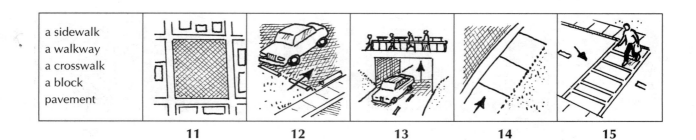

a sidewalk a walkway a crosswalk a block pavement				
	11	12	13	14	15

UNDERSTAND: **Negative Questions**

Questions are generally asked in the affirmative. Negative questions are often used to express a sense of surprise.

Can't you speak Italian? (I thought you could).

Negative questions anticipate a particular response which is usually negative.

Can't you speak Italian?   No, I can't.

Affirmative responses are also possible, but they are often accompanied by expressions such as **of course**, which underline the contradiction between the expected response (negative) and the reality (positive).

Can't you speak Italian?   Yes, **of course** I can.

A. Match the questions to the answers.

1. Can't you swim?
2. Haven't you ever been to New York?
3. Shouldn't she have reserved tickets in advance?
4. Didn't they have breakfast this morning?
5. Hadn't he graduated when he left the country?
6. Wasn't that surprising news we got at the meeting?
7. Won't the weather affect their plans?
8. Wouldn't you like to relax on a desert island?
9. Wasn't that Simon who called so late last night?
10. Haven't they heard that joke before?
11. Can't we return the merchandise if it is defective?
12. Haven't you finished reading that book?
13. Didn't the medical supplies arrive by air?
14. Weren't all the students in the class invited?
15. Haven't all the wedding arrangements been completed?

a) Everyone received an invitation but not everyone could come.
b) No. We don't have a list of the groom's family yet.
c) I don't think so. No planes have landed here today.
d) Of course. I go to the pool every day.
e) Not necessarily. You can usually get tickets at the door.
f) No. They got up late and didn't have time.

a grate					
a workhole cover					
a ramp					
a trash receptacle					
litter					
	16	**17**	**18**	**19**	**20**

g) I've always wanted to go but it's kind of an expensive trip.

h) Sure it will. They'll have to postpone the game.

i) Not really. Most people were expecting bad news.

j) He was trying to finish but he had two courses left.

k) I sure would. I really need to get away.

l) Of course. This is a new book from the library.

m) I'm sure everyone at the party has heard it by now.

n) No. I think it was someone from the car pool.

o) Of course. It is all under guarantee.

B. Write negative questions. Use the appropriate auxiliary verb. Use contractions.

John has never seen the Great Wall of China.

Hasn't John ever seen the Great Wall of China?

1. Mike works in the accounting department.
2. Keiko and Mei live in a high-rise apartment.
3. Annie never walks to work in the morning.
4. Tim and Joan couldn't make it to the party.
5. Min Hee is interested in learning judo.
6. Alberto doesn't like swimming in the ocean.
7. The game was cancelled because of rain.
8. Maria had had supper when she got here.
9. The weather forecast is never good on weekends.
10. Kwong hasn't had any time off this week.
11. The janitor cleaned the graffiti off the wall.
12. The restaurant has a neon sign.
13. We met a lot of people at the party.
14. We should leave for home before it's too late.
15. Dan has changed since we last saw him.

a neon sign a poster a billboard graffiti a mural					
	21	22	23	24	25

UNDERSTAND: **WH-Information Questions**

Wh-information questions request a response that includes some specific type of information.

Apply the same rules for question form word order as for yes/no questions. Use a WH-question word to indicate the type of information you are requesting. Put the WH-question word at the beginning of the question.

> **Where do they live?**

When	time	When does the bus leave?
Where	location	Where do you live?
Who	people	Who did you meet?
Why	reason	Why are you late?
What	things	What did you lose?

What + noun		
time		What time does the bus leave?
kind (of)		What kind of music is it?
size		What size do you wear?
colour, etc.		What colour are his eyes?

Which + noun	choice	Which book did you buy?
		Which person did you see?
		Which one do you want?

How	manner	How did you get here?
How much + noun	quantity (non count)	How much fun did you have?
How many + noun	quantity (count)	How many movies did you see?

How + adverb		
often		How often does it leave?
soon		How soon does it start?
slowly, etc.		How slowly does it move?

How + adjective		
big		How big is the house?
tall		How tall is the building?
smart		How smart is a monkey?
hungry		How hungry is a lion?
far		How far is New York?
expensive, etc.		How expensive is the ring?

How long (for time)		How long have you lived here? (Two years)
How old (for age)		How old is he? (He's 24.)

a telephone pole
a flag pole
a fountain
a revolving door
a bus shelter

| 26 | 27 | 28 | 29 | 30 |

> **TEACHER'S BOX:** **How long** can also be used to ask about distance: "How long was the race?" "3 kilometres." **How old** can also be used to ask a general question about age: "How old are they?" "They are kids. They're young."

A. Complete the questions with the correct auxiliary verb.

Where (is/~~will~~) the meeting tomorrow going to be held?

1. How many criminals (have/were) been caught by the police?
2. Which kind of paint (is/does) selling best this week?
3. What (were/are) you doing when I phoned you last night?
4. When (do/are) they leaving for their vacation?
5. Where (did/have) you been all my life?
6. Why (were/can) you so late for the party?
7. Who (have/were) you been talking to on the phone?
8. How often (does/is) she exercise at the health club?
9. What kind of shoes (were/have) been most popular?
10. Where (have/did) she learn to speak Japanese so well?

B. Write 15 WH-information questions based on the information in the text below. Use a separate sheet of paper.

Coffee, Coke, and Clorets

by *Michael Castelman*

When was the last time you used a healing herb? You may not realize it, but you use herbs that have medicinal properties all the time. We all do. Perhaps you started your day with a cup of coffee or tea. Coffee is not only America's favourite morning stimulant, but scientists have shown it's also an effective bronchial decongestant. Tea is less stimulating than coffee, but it has also been found to be an effective decongestant. And it's a good source of fluoride, so it would help in preventing tooth decay.

Do you enjoy soft drinks? Most of today's carbonated beverages were originally herbal medicines. Thousands of years ago, the ancient Chinese drank ginger tea for indigestion, a use supported by modern science. During Elizabethan times, the English developed their own ginger-based stomach soother, ginger beer, which evolved into today's ginger ale.

Coca-Cola began as an attempt to develop an herbal headache remedy. Coke was invented in the 1880s by an Atlanta pharmacist who stocked the tropical kola nut because

a siren					
a fire escape					
a railing					
a construction crane					
a street sign	31	32	33	34	35

nineteenth-century physicians prescribed it to treat respiratory aliments. Not too long ago, an article in the *Journal of the American Medical Association* suggested giving cola drinks to children with asthma as preventive medication.

The last time you dined out, did your plate come with a sprig of parsley? Parsley garnishes are another echo of herbal healing. People used to munch this herb to freshen their breath after meals. Parsley is high in the breath-sweetening plant pigment chlorophyll—the Clor in Clorets

breath mints and one of the active ingredients in Certs.

And speaking of restaurants, perhaps your last check arrived with an after-dinner mint. These candies harken back to ancient times, when people sipped mint tea after feasts to settle their stomachs, another traditional medicinal use supported by modern science.

(Excerpted from *The Healing Herbs* ©1991, by Michael Castelman. Permission to reprint by Rodale Press, Inc., Emmaus, PA 18098.)

UNDERSTAND: **"Who" and "What" as Subjects in Questions**

Generally question words have the role of **object** in the sentence.

What did you see?

You saw **what**
s   v   o

you	= subject
did see	= verb
what	= object

Who(m) did you meet?

You met **whom**
s   v   o

you	= subject
did meet	= verb
who	= object

In some questions, **who** and **what** have the role of **subject** in the sentence. Since it is not possible to use another subject in the sentence, the question word (subject) is followed directly by the verb.

What happened?
s   v

Who saw the accident?
s   v   o

Language in Transition

The form **whom** indicates the objective case. However, in contemporary English, the form **who** is more commonly used, even for the objective case.

---

an overpass
pigeons
a bicycle stand
a news-stand
a park bench

| 36 | 37 | 38 | 39 | 40 |

> **TEACHER'S BOX:** The word order in a question can obscure the function of the elements of a sentence. If we look at the answer to the question, we can see the sentence elements more easily.
>
> Who saw the accident? Someone saw the accident.
>   **S**   **V**   **O**   **S**   **V**   **O**

A. Write questions using the question words **who** and **what** as subjects in the sentences.

The ball got lost. **What got lost?**
The coach got angry. **Who got angry?**

1. A traffic accident happened here.
2. The police arrived quickly.
3. They took careful notes.
4. An ambulance was called.
5. The driver was in shock.
6. The injured were taken to the hospital.
7. Newspaper reporters arrived on the scene.
8. Pictures were taken of the scene.
9. Photos were published in the paper.
10. Many people read about it the next day.

B. Complete the questions using **what** or **who**. Use **what** and **who** as the subject or object, according to the context.

1. Her brand new bicycle got stolen. What…?
2. The police found her wallet. Who…?
3. The police found her wallet. What…?
4. A courier will bring the package tomorrow. What…?
5. A courier will bring the package tomorrow. Who…?
6. The car got towed away an hour ago. What…?
7. Nancy is getting engaged this month. Who…?
8. She cooked a special dinner for the family. What…?
9. They planned to visit many museums in Paris. What…?
10. Many people participated in the meeting. Who…?
11. A famous writer lived in this house. Who…?
12. His speech drew a lot of applause. What…?
13. John caused the accident by speeding. Who…?
14. The speaker was given a round of applause. What…?
15. The speaker was given a round of applause. Who…?

a squirrel
a subway
a street lamp
a streetcar
a double-decker bus

    41   42   43   44   45

UNDERSTAND: **Questions with "Like"**

There are three types of questions in English that use the word **like**. Each type uses **like** in a different way.

a) **Like** is the main verb and it is used to inquire about personal preference. Put the subject between the auxiliary verb and the main verb.

What do you like?   I like music.

Who(m) do you like?   I like Annabel.

b) **Like** is used after the main verb **be** and is used to mean how something is. It is used to request information about abstract characteristics such as emotions or atmosphere.

What is Annabel like?   She is sensitive and intelligent.

What is Montreal like?   It has cold winters but a lively atmosphere.

c) **Like** is used in the phrase **looks like** to mean "resemble." It is used to inquire about physical characteristics.

What does Annabel look like?   She is tall with red hair.

    She looks like her mother.

What does a crocodile look like?   It looks like an alligator. It is big and green with sharp teeth.

A. Match the questions with appropriate answers.

1. What does a zebra look like?
2. What is Canada like?
3. What do teenagers like?
4. What is New York like?
5. What does a moose look like?
6. What is a sloth like?
7. What kind of food do you like?
8. What are your cousins like?
9. What do your cousins look like?
10. What does an elephant look like?

a) I'm a vegetarian.
b) a very large deer with huge antlers
c) They are really friendly.
d) It's exciting and dangerous.
e) a few acres of snow
f) They all have black hair and blue eyes.
g) a horse wearing striped pyjamas
h) Very lazy. It sleeps 20 hours a day.
i) It has big ears, a trunk, and tusks.
j) loud music

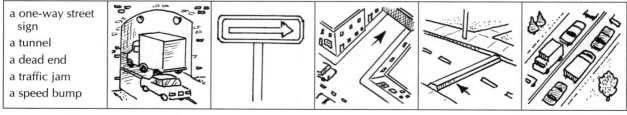

a one-way street sign				
a tunnel				
a dead end				
a traffic jam				
a speed bump				
46	47	48	49	50

B. Make questions that match the answers below. Write questions with **what + like**.

1. Leo is tall with a beard, moustache, and glasses.
2. Mieke is nice and she has a great sense of humour.
3. Steve enjoys listening to jazz and pop music.
4. Charles likes travelling to distant countries.
5. It's an exciting city with many good restaurants.
6. I'm an extremely curious kind of person.
7. Carolyn absolutely loves to go windsurfing.
8. Musicians are generally emotional people.
9. Annabel is fun. She is always the life of the party.
10. The Empire State Building resembles any other skyscraper.

Vocabulary Challenge

Twenty Questions

Work with a partner. Answers these questions quickly, without turning back to the pictures.

1. What shades a balcony from the sun?
2. What can you use to pass from one building to another without going outdoors?
3. What kind of writing is found on walls?
4. What does a fire escape look like?
5. What is used for advertising outdoors?
6. What is used to put up a flag?
7. What can you hold on to when you go down stairs?
8. Where can we make phone calls when we are away from home?
9. What can you use to enter or leave a building without pulling on a door?
10. Where can a wheelchair have easy access to a sidewalk?
11. What kind of birds do we find in a city?
12. What kind of building has many storeys?
13. What kind of sign is easy to see at night?
14. What kind of picture is painted on a wall?
15. What makes noise on a fire engine?
16. What are two places where you can park you car?
17. What often happens at rush hour?
18. Where can you wait for a bus without getting wet?
19. Where should you cross a street?
20. What is used to carry building material to the top of a skyscraper?

Ten-Minute Grammar Games

Puzzles

Focus: Review questions.

Students work in pairs to solve the puzzles.

1. Marta used to celebrate her birthday in the middle of summer, but now she celebrates her birthday in the middle of winter. How can this be?
2. Which weighs more, a kilogram of apples or a kilogram of feathers?
3. If a plane crashed on the border of the United States and Canada, where would the survivors be buried?
4. A person had two coins with a value of 30 cents, but one of the coins was not a quarter (25 cents). What two coins did the person have?
5. If you can buy a dozen 46-cent stamps for $5.52, how much does one stamp cost?
6. Yesterday I had $2 million. At 2:00 today I had $200 000 in my hand, but now I need to borrow $20 from my friend. What is my job?

Test Yourself

A. Look at the questions and complete the answers. Use short answers.

Do you know what time the movie starts?   **No, I don't.**

1. Do you want to eat in a restaurant? Yes, _____.
2. Can we meet on the corner at eight o'clock? No, _____.
3. Are you still living on Sherbrooke Street? No, _____.
4. Did they remember meeting you before? Yes, _____.
5. Have they lived abroad for long? No, _____.
6. Has the dinner party been postponed? No, _____.
7. Would you live in France if you could? Yes, _____.
8. Were the children supervised this afternoon? Yes, _____.
9. Did the doctor prescribe antibiotics? No, _____.
10. Is the embassy still in the same building? Yes, _____.
11. Have any of the monthly bills been paid yet? No, _____.
12. Are you interested in going to Toronto next week? No, _____.
13. Had he finished working when you picked him up? Yes, _____.
14. Has the ad for the sublet been put in the paper? No, _____.
15. Have they made any new friends at school this year? Yes, _____.

180

B. Write question using the WH-question words provided.

1. They got lost in the woods when they went hiking. (where)
2. They were able to buy a sailboat by getting a bank loan. (how)
3. Some people left the reception early because they were tired. (why)
4. They visited their parents every second weekend and at special holidays. (how often)
5. The holiday will last until they run out of money. (how long)
6. The youngest member of the orchestra gave the best performance. (who)
7. They have chosen antique furniture for their new house. (what kind)
8. The car broke down just as they were driving through the desert. (when)
9. The explosion was caused by a gas leak. (what)
10. We bought an enormous ice cream sundae at the fair. (how big)
11. They were married in the chapel at the college. (where)
12. My friends and I have arranged to meet at six o'clock. (when)
13. We have chosen the apartment on the ground floor. (which)
14. The university turned many students away at registration. (how many)
15. They will get to the other side of the lake by swimming. (how)

C. Choose the most appropriate answer for each question.

1. What does Keiko like?   friendly   sushi   short
2. What are the Lopez twins like?   boys   shy   Mexico
3. What does Cliff like best?   sailing   tall   sensitive
4. What does Paris look like?   France   elegant   Rome
5. What does Marta like?   pretty   reading   intelligent
6. What is Elynor like?   intelligent   blond   Canadian
7. What does Yolanda look like?   sincere   attractive   jogging
8. What are your parents like?   old   music   strict
9. What is your aerobics workout like?   easy   strong   fitness
10. What does your dog look like?   bones   shaggy   fierce

Score for Test Yourself: _____

40

Vocabulary Answers

1. a balcony
2. a roof terrace
3. a skyscraper
4. a high-rise
5. an awning
6. a parking lot
7. a phone booth
8. a fire hydrant
9. a courier
10. a parking meter
11. a block
12. pavement
13. a walkway
14. a sidewalk
15. a crosswalk
16. a ramp
17. litter
18. a workhole cover
19. a trash receptacle
20. a grate
21. a mural
22. a billboard
23. graffiti
24. a neon sign
25. a poster
26. a bus shelter
27. a fountain
28. a telephone pole
29. a revolving door
30. a flagpole
31. a construction crane
32. a railing
33. a fire escape
34. a street sign
35. a siren
36. a bicycle stand
37. a park bench
38. pigeons
39. an overpass
40. a news-stand
41. a streetcar
42. a subway
43. a double-decker bus
44. a squirrel
45. a street lamp
46. a tunnel
47. a one-way street
48. a dead end
49. a speed bump
50. a traffic jam

TOEFL® Practice Exercises

You have 25 minutes to complete these exercises. When you complete Part A, continue to Part B. An answer sheet is provided on page 197.

Part A

Choose the phrase that best completes the sentence. Blacken the letter that corresponds to your answer on the answer sheet.

Example: Contestants have been told that every entry _____ with their names and addresses in order to be considered for the prize.

(a) must have been labelled
(b) must has to be labelled
(c) must to be labelled
(d) must be labelled

   (A) (B) (C) (D)

1. In the book, _____, the central character is travelling back to his boyhood home to make peace with his aged mother.
   (a) based closely on the author's own life
   (b) is based closely on the author's own life
   (c) which based closely on the author's own life
   (d) which bases closely on the author's own life

2. When the sun _____ and a total eclipse takes place, you can witness a solar corona.
   (a) blocked out the moon
   (b) is blocked out by the moon
   (c) is blocking out the moon
   (d) blocks out by the moon

3. Since they are very concerned about making the right decision, _____ wait a little longer to avoid a mistake.
   - (a) they had rather
   - (b) they rather
   - (c) they would rather
   - (d) they are rather

4. Since my father likes to do things with his hands, he _____ all our furniture by himself.
   - (a) has bought
   - (b) has chosen
   - (c) has done
   - (d) has made

5. The store announced that one cent _____ to a charitable organization for every dollar that is spent in its toy department.
   - (a) will donate
   - (b) will be donated
   - (c) will be donate
   - (d) will be donating

6. A quiet campout in the wilderness turned into a _____ nightmare for the victims of an unprovoked grizzly bear attack.
   - (a) be afraid
   - (b) afraid
   - (c) frightened
   - (d) frightening

7. Georgia _____ her hair cut in an expensive salon, but she wasn't completely satisfied with the results.
   - (a) is having
   - (b) will have
   - (c) has
   - (d) had

8. When our neighbour showed us pictures of her mother, we realized that the two of them really _____ each other.
   - (a) are like
   - (b) seems like
   - (c) look like
   - (d) likes

9. Because of the cast of fine actors, the play we saw last night at the national theatre was _____ we had seen in ages.
   - (a) the most interested
   - (b) the most interesting
   - (c) the more interesting
   - (d) highly interesting

10. After decades _____ and contaminated with pollutants, the Aral Sea has shrunk and is no longer the fourth largest body of fresh water in the world.
    (a) of being neglected
    (b) to be neglected
    (c) from be neglected
    (d) of been neglected

11. The bus company representative would not say how many of the new security agents _____ on the buses.
    (a) would been used
    (b) were using
    (c) were being use
    (d) would be used

12. The speaker we had invited was so convincing that she _____ something to the charity she represented.
    (a) got everyone contribute
    (b) made everyone to contribute
    (c) got everyone to contribute
    (d) had everyone to contribute

13. In some countries cigarettes can be purchased by anyone, while in other countries they _____ adults.
    (a) only can be sold for
    (b) can only be sold to
    (c) only sells to
    (d) can sell only for

14. Biologists have been saying for five years now that fish catches _____ in the waters around Greenland.
    (a) should be reduce
    (b) should have been reduce
    (c) should be reducing
    (d) should be reduced

15. The police chief said that the new surveillance techniques would make it difficult for pickpockets to know if and when they _____.
    (a) was being watching
    (b) were watching
    (c) were being watched
    (d) were watched

Part B

One of the underlined grammar points in each sentence is incorrect. Blacken the number of the error on the answer sheet.

Example: The report was <u>prepared</u>[A] by a task force <u>headed</u>[B] by <u>the</u>[C] transport minister and several of <u>its</u>[D] assistants.

(A) (B) (C) (D)

16. In the <u>days</u>[A] before the stunt, bets <u>was being</u>[B] taken on whether it was really possible <u>to walk</u>[C] across Niagara Falls <u>on a tightrope</u>[D].

17. The <u>best</u>[A] drawings will <u>be judging</u>[B] by a group of professional artists and a prize <u>will be</u>[C] awarded <u>to</u>[D] the winning entry.

18. Yellowknife <u>is served</u>[A] by <u>a</u>[B] single highway <u>which is closes</u>[C] during spring breakup, <u>leaving</u>[D] the city without ground transportation.

19. People in <u>that part</u>[A] of the world <u>has experience</u>[B] many <u>earthquakes</u>[C] and are aware of the disastrous results they <u>can have</u>[D].

20. One writer <u>suggesting</u>[A] that the <u>city's</u>[B] isolation has made it a place where <u>anyone</u>[C] can fit in and where class divisions <u>are blurred</u>[D].

21. <u>A</u>[A] series of trails <u>are laid out</u>[B] along the route and pamphlets and maps <u>can to be obtained</u>[C] from the office of the <u>Visitor's</u>[D] Bureau.

22. <u>A lot of</u>[A] comic books that are <u>being published</u>[B] for teenagers and young adults look more <u>interested</u>[C] that they <u>did</u>[D] in the past.

23. Religions and social rites that <u>used to be</u>[A] separate are now <u>being integrated</u>[B] into new <u>belief</u>[C] systems aimed at <u>reclaim</u>[D] spiritual values.

24. The members of the sect <u>were convinced</u>[A] that <u>their</u>[B] leader's power <u>makes</u>[C] them impervious to the bullets <u>fired</u>[D] by their enemies.

25. The request <u>for</u>[A] an interview <u>was be made</u>[B] through the star's agent <u>who</u>[C] asked for a <u>written</u>[D] list of questions in advance.

26. Around the world people <u>has</u>[A] become <u>fascinated</u>[B] with accounts of <u>miraculous</u>[C] apparitions and of statues <u>that</u>[D] are crying or moving.

27. <u>Some</u>[A] people <u>believe</u>[B] that advertising <u>that</u>[C] links cigarettes to fun and good health <u>should be ban</u>[D] by the government.

28. <u>Frightening</u> [A] by the careless attitude toward the environment they see around <u>them</u> [B], girls <u>are getting</u> [C] educated and campaigning <u>for</u> [D] changes in attitude.

29. Studies <u>show</u> [A] that <u>about</u> [B] 7 percent of men and 1 percent <u>of</u> [C] women have been <u>diagnose</u> [D] with antisocial personalities.

30. In a survey <u>conducted</u> [A] last year, 28 percent of Americans <u>say</u> [B] they <u>had</u> [C] voluntarily cut down on the number of cigarettes they <u>smoked</u> [D].

31. It is impossible <u>to remove</u> [A] all stress <u>from</u> [B] our lives, so how <u>we cope</u> [C] with stress is <u>what does make</u> [D] the difference.

32. Mining and tourism <u>are been</u> [A] looked at as alternatives, <u>but</u> [B] fishing <u>has been</u> [C] the mainstay of the economy in Greenland <u>until</u> [D] now.

33. Public institutions <u>such as</u> [A] schools <u>have been offer</u> [B] free subscriptions <u>to</u> [C] television by cable companies in the <u>greater</u> [D] metropolitan area.

34. Teachers <u>using</u> [A] TV have had <u>to choose</u> [B] between <u>aged</u> [C] educational tapes that are sometimes <u>bored</u> [D] or illegal takes of old network programs.

35. Elderly couples have become <u>increasingly</u> [A] more dependent on <u>their</u> [B] pensions <u>as</u> [C] their investments have <u>be eroded</u> [D] in difficult economic times.

36. In the old days, the <u>settler's</u> [A] wooden houses were not permanently <u>connected to</u> [B] the earth so they <u>could be</u> [C] moved <u>easy</u> [D] by horses.

37. A message left on <u>his</u> [A] answering machine <u>told</u> [B] Russia's most <u>celebrating</u> [C] living writer that the plug <u>had been pulled</u> [D] on his television program.

38. The coach <u>was angry</u> [A] because he <u>felt</u> [B] that the members of the water polo team had not <u>been doing</u> [C] <u>enough</u> [D] effort to win the match.

39. When it <u>was suggested</u> [A] that they move to <u>another</u> [B] location, the victims of the <u>volcanic</u> [C] eruption said that they <u>had rather</u> [D] remain in the same area.

40. The police got the <u>alleged</u> [A] arsonist <u>admit</u> [B] that he <u>was</u> [C] the person who <u>had been seen</u> [D] in the vicinity of the fire the night before.

Appendix 1

Spelling Simple Past Tense

2 consonants	add **ed**	work	work**ed**
2 vowels + consonant	add **ed**	need	need**ed**
vowel + **y**	add **ed**	play	play**ed**
consonant + **y**	change **y** to **i** add **ed**	try	tr**ied**
vowel + consonant	double consonant add **ed**	plan	plan**ned**

Not all verbs that end in vowel + consonant double the final letter. Common exceptions are **listened**, **opened**, **answered**.

For pronunciation rules see *Grammar Connections 1*.

Appendix 2

Irregular Past Tense Verbs and Past Participles

Many past participles are the same as the regular or irregular past tense forms. Irregular past participles are shown in bold type below.

Present	Past	Past participle	Present	Past	Past participle
arise	arose	**arisen**	freeze	froze	**frozen**
awake	awoke	**awaken**	get	got	**gotten** (got)
be	was, were	**been**	give	gave	**given**
beat	beat	**beaten**	go	went	**gone**
become	became	**become**	grow	grew	**grown**
begin	began	**begun**	have	had	had
bite	bit	**bitten**	hear	heard	heard
bleed	bled	bled	hide	hid	**hidden**
blow	blew	**blown**	hit	hit	hit
break	broke	**broken**	hold	held	held
bring	brought	brought	hurt	hurt	hurt
build	built	built	keep	kept	kept
buy	bought	bought	know	knew	**known**
catch	caught	caught	lay	laid	laid
choose	chose	**chosen**	lead	led	led
come	came	**come**	leave	left	left
cost	cost	cost	let	let	let
cut	cut	cut	lie	lay	**lain**
dig	dug	dug	lose	lost	lost
do	did	**done**	make	made	made
draw	drew	**drawn**	mean	meant	meant
drink	drank	**drunk**	meet	met	met
drive	drove	**driven**	pay	paid	paid
eat	ate	**eaten**	put	put	put
fall	fell	**fallen**	read	read	read
feed	fed	fed	ride	rode	**ridden**
feel	felt	felt	ring	rang	**rung**
find	found	found	rise	rose	**risen**
fly	flew	**flown**	run	ran	ran
forbid	forbade	**forbidden**	see	saw	**seen**
forget	forgot	**forgotten**	sell	sold	sold
forgive	forgave	**forgiven**	send	sent	sent

Present	Past	Past participle	Present	Past	Past participle
shake	shook	**shaken**	stink	stank	**stunk**
shine	shone	shone	swear	swore	**sworn**
shoot	shot	shot	swim	swam	**swum**
show	showed	shown	take	took	taken
shrink	shrank	**shrunk**	teach	taught	taught
shut	shut	shut	tear	tore	**torn**
sing	sang	**sung**	tell	told	told
sit	sat	sat	think	thought	thought
sleep	slept	slept	throw	threw	**thrown**
speak	spoke	**spoken**	understand	understood	understood
spread	spread	spread	wake	woke	**woken**
spring	sprang	**sprung**	wear	wore	**worn**
stand	stood	stood	win	won	won
steal	stole	**stolen**	write	wrote	**written**

Appendix 3

Common Stative Verbs

be	need
believe	owe
belong to	own
contain	realize
cost	recognize
deserve	remember
dislike	see
feel	seem
forget	smell
hate	sound
have	suppose
hear	taste
imagine	think
include	understand
know	want
like	weigh
love	wish
mean	

TOEFL® Practice Exercises Answer Sheet

Part A

Choose the phrase that best completes the sentence. Blacken the letter that corresponds to the answer.

1. (A) (B) (C) (D)
2. (A) (B) (C) (D)
3. (A) (B) (C) (D)
4. (A) (B) (C) (D)
5. (A) (B) (C) (D)
6. (A) (B) (C) (D)
7. (A) (B) (C) (D)
8. (A) (B) (C) (D)
9. (A) (B) (C) (D)
10. (A) (B) (C) (D)
11. (A) (B) (C) (D)
12. (A) (B) (C) (D)
13. (A) (B) (C) (D)
14. (A) (B) (C) (D)
15. (A) (B) (C) (D)

Score 15

Part B

Blacken the letter that corresponds to the error in the sentence.

16. (A) (B) (C) (D)
17. (A) (B) (C) (D)
18. (A) (B) (C) (D)
19. (A) (B) (C) (D)
20. (A) (B) (C) (D)
21. (A) (B) (C) (D)
22. (A) (B) (C) (D)
23. (A) (B) (C) (D)
24. (A) (B) (C) (D)
25. (A) (B) (C) (D)
26. (A) (B) (C) (D)
27. (A) (B) (C) (D)
28. (A) (B) (C) (D)
29. (A) (B) (C) (D)
30. (A) (B) (C) (D)
31. (A) (B) (C) (D)
32. (A) (B) (C) (D)
33. (A) (B) (C) (D)
34. (A) (B) (C) (D)
35. (A) (B) (C) (D)
36. (A) (B) (C) (D)
37. (A) (B) (C) (D)
38. (A) (B) (C) (D)
39. (A) (B) (C) (D)
40. (A) (B) (C) (D)

Score 25

TOEFL® Practice Exercises Answer Sheet

Part A

Choose the phrase that best completes the sentence. Blacken the letter that corresponds to the answer.

1. (A) (B) (C) (D)
2. (A) (B) (C) (D)
3. (A) (B) (C) (D)
4. (A) (B) (C) (D)
5. (A) (B) (C) (D)
6. (A) (B) (C) (D)
7. (A) (B) (C) (D)
8. (A) (B) (C) (D)
9. (A) (B) (C) (D)
10. (A) (B) (C) (D)
11. (A) (B) (C) (D)
12. (A) (B) (C) (D)
13. (A) (B) (C) (D)
14. (A) (B) (C) (D)
15. (A) (B) (C) (D)

Score 15

Part B

Blacken the letter that corresponds to the error in the sentence.

16. (A) (B) (C) (D)
17. (A) (B) (C) (D)
18. (A) (B) (C) (D)
19. (A) (B) (C) (D)
20. (A) (B) (C) (D)
21. (A) (B) (C) (D)
22. (A) (B) (C) (D)
23. (A) (B) (C) (D)
24. (A) (B) (C) (D)
25. (A) (B) (C) (D)
26. (A) (B) (C) (D)
27. (A) (B) (C) (D)
28. (A) (B) (C) (D)
29. (A) (B) (C) (D)
30. (A) (B) (C) (D)
31. (A) (B) (C) (D)
32. (A) (B) (C) (D)
33. (A) (B) (C) (D)
34. (A) (B) (C) (D)
35. (A) (B) (C) (D)
36. (A) (B) (C) (D)
37. (A) (B) (C) (D)
38. (A) (B) (C) (D)
39. (A) (B) (C) (D)
40. (A) (B) (C) (D)

Score 25

TOEFL® Practice Exercises Answer Sheet

Part A

Choose the phrase that best completes the sentence. Blacken the letter that corresponds to the answer.

1. (A) (B) (C) (D)
2. (A) (B) (C) (D)
3. (A) (B) (C) (D)
4. (A) (B) (C) (D)
5. (A) (B) (C) (D)
6. (A) (B) (C) (D)
7. (A) (B) (C) (D)
8. (A) (B) (C) (D)
9. (A) (B) (C) (D)
10. (A) (B) (C) (D)
11. (A) (B) (C) (D)
12. (A) (B) (C) (D)
13. (A) (B) (C) (D)
14. (A) (B) (C) (D)
15. (A) (B) (C) (D)

Score 15

Part B

Blacken the letter that corresponds to the error in the sentence.

16. (A) (B) (C) (D)
17. (A) (B) (C) (D)
18. (A) (B) (C) (D)
19. (A) (B) (C) (D)
20. (A) (B) (C) (D)
21. (A) (B) (C) (D)
22. (A) (B) (C) (D)
23. (A) (B) (C) (D)
24. (A) (B) (C) (D)
25. (A) (B) (C) (D)
26. (A) (B) (C) (D)
27. (A) (B) (C) (D)
28. (A) (B) (C) (D)
29. (A) (B) (C) (D)
30. (A) (B) (C) (D)
31. (A) (B) (C) (D)
32. (A) (B) (C) (D)
33. (A) (B) (C) (D)
34. (A) (B) (C) (D)
35. (A) (B) (C) (D)
36. (A) (B) (C) (D)
37. (A) (B) (C) (D)
38. (A) (B) (C) (D)
39. (A) (B) (C) (D)
40. (A) (B) (C) (D)

Score 25

Index

200

Test Yourself Answers

Unit 1

(Page 14)

A. Cross out the incorrect forms on the list of past participles.

1. come/~~came~~
2. ~~set~~/sat
3. ~~chose~~/chosen
4. grown/~~grewn~~
5. ~~rodden~~/ridden
6. felt/~~fallen~~
7. caught/~~catcht~~
8. drawn/~~drewn~~
9. forbidden/~~forbaden~~
10. shrunk/~~shrunken~~

(Page 14)

B. Write questions that correspond to these answers, using appropriate WH-question words or phrases.

1. Where did they go for their summer holidays last year?
2. What did Peter catch the last time he went fishing?
3. How did Gabriel feel during the long boat ride yesterday?
4. What did the students hear?
5. Where did they camp on their last hiking trip?
6. When did the hotel receptionist wake us up?
7. What did you feel when you returned to North America?
8. Why did they get sunburned?
9. How far did they drive across the desert?
10. How many accidents did the football player have last season?

(Page 14)

C. Choose the simple past or the present perfect form of the verb.

1. took
2. has bitten
3. has never bought
4. rose
5. have found
6. Has (anyone here) ever gone
7. went out
8. forgot
9. have never seen
10. caught

(Page 15)

D. Find the errors and correct them. If the sentence is correct put a check.

1. We have never seen…
2. Haven't you ever tried…
3. Correct
4. My friend hasn't ever taken/has never taken…
5. Has your family ever visited…
6. They haven't ever been/have never been…
7. Correct
8. Hasn't anyone ever ridden…
9. Correct
10. Correct

Unit 2

(Page 25)

A. Write these sentences using the present continuous form of the verb.

1. John has been managing an all-night gas station.
2. Suzanne has been training for the Olympic Games.
3. Maria has been teaching swimming at the YWCA.
4. Lili and Chen have been renting an apartment downtown.
5. Max and Bob have been building a boat in the basement.

202

6. The government has been trying to discourage smoking.
7. Our school has been offering scholarships to good students.
8. My grandmother has been baking cookies for the bazaar on Saturday.
9. Julia has been taking a French course this summer.
10. Marta has been sewing a dress for her younger sister.

(Page 25)

B. Complete the dialogue with the simple past, present perfect or present perfect continuous.
1. haven't seen
2. I've been
3. graduated
4. have you finished
5. got
6. I've been looking
7. Have you had
8. I've had
9. have you been doing
10. haven't found
11. have been working
12. have you been working
13. worked
14. has he been doing
15. has been working
16. have been going out
17. haven't talked
18. We've been
19. I've missed
20. It's been great (It was great)

(Page 26)

C. Complete the explanations with the correct form of the present perfect continuous.
1. g   a) has been getting
2. d   b) has been studying
3. j   c) has not been missing
4. e   d) has been going to bed
5. b   e) have not been doing
6. i   f) has not been cleaning
7. c   g) has not been studying
8. f   h) has been going
9. a   i) has been expecting
10. h   j) has not been setting

Unit 3

(Page 38)

A. Replace the nouns in bold with gerunds that mean the same thing.
1. working   3. writing
2. waiting   4. living

5. switching jobs   8. growing up
6. improving his diet   9. staying
7. watching TV   10. travelling

(Page 38)

B. Fill in the correct prepositions.
1. of   6. at
2. on   7. about
3. at   8. in
4. of   9. on
5. about   10. with

(Page 38)

C. Complete the sentences with the gerund or the infinitive form of the verb.
1. going   6. to drive
2. getting up   7. to go
3. wearing   8. to support
4. to take   9. leaving
5. to be   10. meeting

(Page 39)

D. Some sentences have errors. Find the errors and correct them.
1. didn't let her play
2. makes the students practise
3. did not let the tourists photograph
4. Correct
5. Correct
6. made everyone who arrived late wait
7. let the students bring
8. Correct
9. makes her students memorize
10. Correct

Unit 4

(Page 51)

A. Write tag questions to complete the sentences.
1. isn't she?   9. is he?
2. doesn't he?   10. wasn't it?
3. have you?   11. doesn't it?
4. isn't it?   12. isn't it?
5. would he/she?   13. won't we?
6. could they?   14. didn't it?
7. didn't they?   15. do you ?
8. didn't she?

(Page 52)

B. Complete the short dialogues with **too** or **so**.
1. too   6. so
2. too   7. too
3. so   8. so
4. so   9. so
5. too   10. too

(Page 52)

C. Agree with the following statements with **so** or **neither**.

1. So do I.
2. Neither have I.
3. So have I.
4. So do I.
5. Neither did I.
6. Neither will I.
7. So should I.
8. So did I.
9. So would I.
10. So am I.
11. So can I.
12. Neither did I.
13. Neither do I.
14. So do I.
15. So did I.

Unit 6

(Page 72)

A. Write the past perfect form of the following verbs.

1. had gone
2. had known
3. had become
4. had worn
5. had taken
6. had had
7. had found
8. had drunk
9. had given
10. had been
11. had eaten
12. had understood
13. had thrown
14. had driven
15. had spoken
16. had stolen
17. had woken
18. had begun
19. had broken
20. had blown

(Page 72)

B. Put the verbs in brackets in the correct tenses.

1. When the guests had gone / the hosts cleaned up
2. After they had eaten / they went
3. When the speaker had finished / everyone applauded
4. Before the exam ended / the students had handed in
5. After the meeting had begun / someone knocked
6. The team left / after the coach had announced
7. By the time we arrived / the other guests had gone
8. After they had checked / they gave us
9. Before I went / I had put on
10. The team had put on / the game started

(Page 72)

C. Complete the sentences with **hope** or **wish**.

1. wishes
2. hope
3. hopes
4. wish
5. hopes
6. wish
7. wishes
8. wish
9. hope
10. wishes

Unit 7

(Page 86)

A. Put the verbs in brackets in the correct tense.

1. will be
2. don't have
3. are
4. won't pass
5. won't hear
6. won't be
7. is
8. doesn't get
9. won't have
10. will speak

(Page 87)

B. Complete the sentences using the correct form of the verb in brackets.

1. got
2. had
3. spoke
4. asked
5. applied
6. entered
7. saw
8. won
9. had
10. knew
11. took
12. knew
13. drove
14. didn't break
15. lived

(Page 87)

C. Complete the sentences using the correct form of the verb in brackets.

1. would have quit
2. would have finished
3. would have had
4. would have been
5. would have felt
6. would have helped
7. would have got (gotten)
8. would have graduated
9. would have enjoyed
10. would have arrived

(Page 87)

D. Put the verbs in the correct tense.

1. would not have gone
2. know
3. paid
4. were (was)
5. wouldn't have taken

Unit 8

(Page 102)

A. Choose the present or past form of the verbs to complete the sentences.

1. must have been held up
2. may have forgotten
3. should be
4. must have happened
5. may stay
6. might have missed

204

7. should arrive
8. may be lost
9. must have slept in
10. could have

(Page 103)

B. Change the verbs in bold to the negative.
1. might not have been / might not be
2. could not have made
3. may not have remembered
4. should not have been
5. could not have been
6. might not have come
7. may not have arrived
8. could not have been
9. may not have met
10. might not have brought

(Page 103)

C. Complete the sentences with **must** + verb or **must have been** + verb.
1. must have been
2. must have felt
3. must have
4. must be
5. must have broken
6. must have wanted
7. must need
8. must have postponed
9. must have run out
10. must have been

(Page 103)

D. Choose the affirmative or negative form of **had better**.
1. I'd better report it
2. I'd better take it
3. I'd better not be late again
4. I'd better not fall asleep again
5. I'd better not miss one again
6. I'd better spend
7. I'd better stop smoking
8. I'd better not have desserts
9. I'd better take some time off
10. I'd better not forget it again

Unit 9

(Page 117)

A. Change the statements into direct speech. Make all the necessary changes.
1. The doctor said, "The patient needs to be hospitalized."
2. The newscaster reported, "The forest fire is under control."
3. The meteorologist announced, "There is a tornado warning."
4. The bank manager said, "Interest rates will go up this week."
5. The ballet teacher said, "Everyone needs to practise more."
6. The photographer said, "I need to take more pictures."
7. The police officer said, "You need to fasten your seat belts."
8. The officer manager said, "The new computer system will be installed soon."
9. The air-traffic controller said, "Some flights will be delayed."
10. The fashion designer said, "The autumn styles are exceptional this year."

(Page 117)

B. Change the sentences into indirect speech. Make all the necessary changes.
1. They said that they had been to Europe before.
2. He answered that a two-way ticket would be cheaper.
3. The guide explained that we would have to wait for our turn.
4. They said that they would try to take better care next time.
5. She said that the party was going to be a big hit.
6. The teenagers promised that they would be home before 11:00.
7. Our teacher explained that we would all pass if we studied hard.
8. They said that they were too tired to do any more work.
9. He said that the water was too cold to swim in.
10. They said that they had to be home in time for dinner.

(Page 118)

C. Change the imperative statements into indirect speech with **they said**. Make any necessary changes.
1. They said to turn right at the street corner.
2. They said not to cross the street without looking.
3. They said not to worry about the math exam.
4. They said to remember to bring our passports when we came there.
5. They said to try to guess, if we weren't sure of the answer.
6. They said to wait until other passengers had left the aircraft.
7. They said not to forget to brush my (our) teeth before I (we) went to bed.
8. They said not to forget to turn off the lights before we left.
9. They said to check the price before we (I) bought those peaches.
10. They said to help ourselves to anything we saw there.

(Page 118)

D. Choose **say** or **tell** and put it in the appropriate tense.

1. told
2. say
3. told
4. say
5. tells
6. told
7. said
8. told
9. say
10. told

Unit 11
(Page 138)

A. Change these sentence to the passive voice.
1. Everyone was complimented for their good work.
2. The papers were distributed late.
3. All the windows in the building will be changed.
4. Activities for senior citizens are organized at the rec centre.
5. The students' journals were collected every month.
6. The photocopy machine will be repaired tomorrow.
7. The plans will be presented at the next meeting.
8. Teenagers are expected to be home by 11:00.
9. Only two pieces of music were played last night.
10. The carpets are cleaned twice a year.

(Page 138)

B. Choose the active or passive form of the verb to complete the sentences. Use the correct verb tense.

1. was arrested
2. was rescued
3. will be inspected
4. destroyed
5. acquired
6. puts
7. was eliminated
8. will be sworn in
9. will be elected
10. will be checked

(Page 138)

C. Check sentences where it is appropriate to mention the doer. Cross out the **by** phrase where it is not appropriate.

1. by the teacher
2. ✔
3. by the interviewer
4. ✔
5. ✔
6. by the announcer
7. by the teacher
8. by me
9. by people
10. by firefighters

(Page 139)

D. Choose the correct form of the adjective.
1. amazing
2. frustrating
3. tired
4. motivated
5. exhausting
6. relaxed
7. depressing
8. exhilarating
9. discriminating
10. discouraging

Unit 12
(Page 152)

A. Find the errors and correct them. If there is no error put a check.
1. was being built
2. is being renovated
3. are being conducted
4. are being shown
5. Correct
6. are being kept
7. is being questioned
8. Correct
9. is being repaired
10. is being given

(Page 152)

B. Put the following sentences in the passive form. Omit mention of the doer if it is not necessary.

1. A huge celebration has been prepared for the anniversary.
2. A great deal of destruction has been caused by the eruption of the volcano.
3. Those manuscripts have been kept under lock and key for centuries.
4. Very little of the money that was borrowed has been repaid.
5. Only part of the symphony had been finished when Schubert died.
6. Most of the damage had already been cleaned up when we arrived.
7. The building had been completely destroyed by the time the fire department arrived.
8. The picnic had been overrun by a colony of ants by the time we finished eating.
9. All the tickets had been sold by the time we arrived at the theatre.
10. Large sections of the downtown area have been flooded.

(Page 153)

C. Choose the best verb to complete each sentence. Use the passive voice with **be going to**.
1. is going to be sold
2. are going to be put
3. are going to be corrected
4. are going to be towed
5. is going to be invited
6. are going to be taken
7. is going to be taught
8. is going to be held up
9. is going to be met
10. is going to be given

(Page 153)

D. Fill in the blanks with the correct form of the verb in brackets.
1. play
2. waited
3. didn't buy
4. spend
5. speak
6. put in
7. visit
8. have
9. told
10. came back

Unit 13
(Page 165)

A. Complete the sentences by choosing a causer from the list below.

1. the doctor
2. the editor
3. the company
4. the politician
5. the tour guide
6. the conductor
7. the artist
8. the customer
9. the hostess
10. the teacher

(Page 165)

B. Rewrite the sentences omitting mention of the doer.

1. The vacationers had their phone disconnected while they were away.
2. The bus driver had the brakes checked before he took the vehicle on the road.
3. We had our kitchen cupboards painted after we cleaned them.
4. I had my homework checked over very carefully before I gave it to the teacher.
5. Margot had the flowers arranged in an attractive bouquet before she left the store.
6. The young lawyer had her hair cut before she appeared in court.
7. The City of Montreal had the snow cleared before the streets became dangerous.
8. My older brother had the house cleaned before my parents came back from vacation.
9. The airline had the missing baggage loaded on the next flight.
10. The animal lover had his cat vaccinated to protect it from rabies.

(Page 165)

C. Rewrite these sentences using **get** as the causative verb.

1. Janet got John to change the light bulbs.
2. The mother gets the children to wash the dishes.
3. The director got the movie star to act in his new film.
4. The old couple gets the supermarket to deliver their groceries.
5. The kindergarten teacher gets the kids to put away their toys.
6. Max got his father to read him a story before he went to bed.
7. Most schools get their students to recycle paper.
8. The company got all its employees to take computer courses.
9. The baby-sitter got the children to go to bed early.
10. Francisco got his friends to help him move his furniture.

(Page 166)

D. List the activities under **make** or **do**.

Make	Do
a mistake	research
dinner	the dishes
an effort	homework
the bed	the laundry
a deal	exercise
a cake	the shopping
friends	a favour
noise	a good job
money	
enemies	
sense	
reservations	

Unit 14
(Page 179)

A. Look at the questions and complete the answers. Use short answers.

1. Yes, I do.
2. No, we can't.
3. No, I'm not.
4. Yes, they did.
5. No, they haven't.
6. No, it hasn't.
7. Yes, I would.
8. Yes, they were.
9. No, he/she didn't.
10. Yes, it is.
11. No, they haven't.
12. No, I'm not.
13. Yes, he had.
14. No, it hasn't.
15. Yes, they have.

(Page 180)

B. Write questions using the WH-questions words provided.

1. Where did they get lost?
2. How were they able to buy a sailboat?
3. Why did some people leave the reception early?
4. How often did they visit their parents?
5. How long will the holiday last?
6. Who gave the best performance?
7. What kind of furniture have they chosen for their new house?
8. When did the car break down?
9. What caused the explosion?
10. How big was the ice cream sundae?
11. Where were they married?
12. When have you and your friends arranged to meet?
13. Which apartment have you chosen?
14. How many students did the university turn away at registration?
15. How will they get to the other side of the lake?

(Page 180)

C. Choose the most appropriate answer for each question.

1. sushi
2. shy
3. sailing
4. Rome
5. reading
6. intelligent
7. attractive
8. strict
9. easy
10. shaggy

Answer Key

Unit 1

What Do You Know?

(Page 1)

1.	awoken	26.	went
2.	arose	27.	grew
3.	was, were	28.	hid
4.	beaten	29.	know
5.	became	30.	ridden
6.	begin	31.	ring
7.	bitten	32.	risen
8.	blow	33.	ran
9.	broke	34.	saw
10.	brought	35.	shaken
11.	chose	36.	showed
12.	come	37.	shrank
13.	do	38.	sung
14.	drew	39.	speak
15.	drunk	40.	sprang
16.	drive	41.	stolen
17.	ate	42.	stunk
18.	fallen	43.	swore
19.	fly	44.	swum
20.	forbade	45.	taken
21.	forgotten	46.	tore
22.	forgave	47.	throw
23.	freeze	48.	wake
24.	got	49.	worn
25.	given	50.	write

Understand: Simple Past Tense

(Page 4)

A. Complete the sentences with the correct verb.

1.	rode	9.	drove
2.	won	10.	left
3.	taught	11.	paid
4.	spent	12.	bought
5.	spoke	13.	took
6.	met	14.	made
7.	slept	15.	got
8.	fell		

Understand: Simple Past Tense Negative Form

(Page 5)

A. Change the verbs to the negative form.

1. Marianne **didn't like** to go to the beach when she was young.
2. Max **didn't spend** time with his uncle in Brazil during the school year.
3. The airplane **didn't leave** on time because of the hurricane warning.
4. In the 1960s people **didn't need** a visa to travel to the Soviet Union.
5. The diplomat **didn't receive** a warm welcome on his trip to France last week.
6. The tour guide **didn't take** the children to the science museum this morning.
7. The diplomats **didn't stand** in line with the other passengers at customs.
8. My brother **didn't run** in the Boston Marathon this year.
9. The agent **didn't ask** for our boarding passes at the check-in counter.
10. We **didn't drink** fresh fruit juice every time we went to the beach in Mexico.

207

Understand: Simple Past Tense Question Form

Yes/No Questions

(Page 5)

A. Write yes/no questions.
1. Did the employees demand better working conditions?
2. Did our neighbours invite us to come over for dinner?
3. Did the teacher ask the students why they were late?
4. Did Charles find learning Chinese very difficult?
5. Did they pay a lot of money for their airline ticket?
6. Did you wait a long time at the ticket counter?
7. Did Miriam break her mother's favourite vase by accident?
8. Did Leo get malaria when he was travelling in the tropics?
9. Did the train accident occur early yesterday morning?
10. Did he hurt himself while he was working on his car?

WH-Questions

(Page 6)

A. Match the questions and answers.
1.	f	6.	d	11.	n
2.	k	7.	l	12.	o
3.	e	8.	h	13.	m
4.	c	9.	g	14.	b
5.	j	10.	i	15.	a

Understand: Present Perfect Aspect

(Page 7)

A. Complete the sentences with the correct form of the present perfect.
1.	has been	6.	has spoken
2.	have lived	7.	has worked
3.	have known	8.	has gone
4.	have been	9.	has lived
5.	has been	10.	has spoken

Understand: Simple Past Tense vs. Present Perfect Aspect

(Page 8)

A. Choose the simple past or the present perfect form of the verb.
1.	lived	6.	knew
2.	have shared	7.	worked
3.	have worked for	8.	have been
4.	have had	9.	have known
5.	were	10.	had

(Page 9)

B. Complete the story with the verbs indicated.
1.	graduated	9.	has been
2.	have studied	10.	have decided
3.	took	11.	have not decided
4.	has been	12.	have heard
5.	went	13.	have saved
6.	spent	14.	have not mentioned
7.	chose	15.	discussed
8.	have visited		

(Page 9)

C. Answer the questions about the paragraph above.
1. They have decided to study French in France.
2. They graduated from college last month.
3. She has studied French for many years.
4. Her friend has taken two French courses.
5. They went to find out about French courses yesterday.
6. They spent the whole day trying to decide on a school.
7. They finally chose to study at Aix-en-Provence.
8. They have visited Paris several times.
9. They have not decided where to live.
10. They have heard that it is expensive to live in Aix-en-Provence.
11. They have saved a little money.
12. They have not mentioned their plans to their parents.
13. They discussed their plans with their teacher.
14. She recommended that they tell their parents right away.

Understand: Present Perfect and Questions with "Ever"

(Page 10)

A. Choose the best words to complete the questions.
1.	ever eaten	6.	ever attended
2.	ever seen	7.	ever visited
3.	ever given	8.	ever fallen
4.	ever taken	9.	ever thought
5.	ever tried	10.	ever dreamed

Understand: Present Perfect and Negative with "Never"

(Page 10)

A. Complete the sentences with the present perfect form of the verb + **never**
1.	has never driven	6.	have never drunk
2.	have never met	7.	have never met
3.	has never had	8.	has never given
4.	has never swum	9.	has never lost
5.	have never eaten	10.	has never won

Vocabulary Challenge
(Page 11)

Unit 2

Understand: Present Perfect Continuous
Use of Present Perfect Continuous
(Page 18)

A. Find the expressions with dynamic verbs.
1. wait for someone
4. meet someone
6. have a good time
7. see a special boyfriend
10. live in Vancouver
12. study for an exam
13. eat a hamburger
16. speak Turkish
17. work for the government (possible)
19. have a bath

Form of Present Perfect Continuous
(Page 19)

A. Write sentences in the present perfect continuous form using the dynamic (action) verbs from the list in the previous exercise.

Ask the teacher to check the grammar.

Understand: Additional Uses of the Present Perfect Continuous

Actions Finished in Immediate Past Time
(Page 20)

A. Look at the pictures and answer the questions.
1. She's been ironing shirts.
2. He's been vacuuming the carpets.
3. They've been eating cookies.
4. He's been painting.
5. She's been cooking.
6. They've been playing tennis.
7. She's been singing / performing.
8. He's been shopping for food.
9. They've been drying the dishes.
10. They've been swimming.

(Page 21)

B. Match the situation with the question you would ask.
1. j
2. f
3. h
4. i
5. e
6. g
7. b
8. c
9. a
10. d

Recent Habits or Unusual Behaviour
(Page 22)

A. Give reasons for the situations.
1. They haven't been playing well recently / lately.
2. He has been exercising a lot recently / lately.
3. She has been practising in the lab recently / lately.
4. We have been using a microwave recently / lately.
5. They haven't been watching so much TV recently / lately.
6. He has been growing a beard recently / lately.
7. He has been working at two jobs recently / lately.
8. It has been burning everything recently / lately.
9. I have been sneezing a lot recently / lately.
10. He hasn't been studying much recently / lately.

Understand: Present Perfect Continuous – Negative
(Page 23)

A. Match the comments with the explanations.
1. e
2. d
3. g
4. a
5. i
6. b
7. j
8. f
9. c
10. h

Vocabulary Challenge
(Page 24)

toaster	box spring
blender	mattress
microwave	headboard
bottle opener	sheets
can opener	pillows
corkscrew	blankets
curtains	
blinds	
drapes	

Unit 3

Understand: Gerunds as Subjects, Objects, or Complements

(Page 29)

A. Use a gerund to replace the words in bold type.
1. reading
2. lying / telling lies always gets
3. studying
4. exercising
5. visiting Australia / travelling to Australia
6. crying
7. travelling
8. walking / taking a walk
9. joking / telling jokes is
10. dancing
11. preparing is
12. resting / relaxing

(Page 30)

B. Underline the gerunds. Replace the gerunds with appropriate nouns.
1. <u>travelling</u> / trips
2. <u>collecting stamps</u> / stamp collections
3. <u>reading</u> / books and magazines
4. <u>taking language courses</u> / language study
5. <u>living</u> / urban life
6. <u>sending instant correspondence</u> / a fax
7. <u>working</u> / summer jobs
8. <u>having difficulty sleeping</u> / insomnia
9. <u>obsessive dieting</u> / a strict diet
10. <u>twitching and shaking</u> / agitation

Understand: Gerunds as Subjects and Objects

(Page 30)

A. Complete the sentence with the appropriate verb from the list below.
1. wearing
2. exercising
3. travelling
4. relaxing
5. diving
6. taking
7. learning
8. postponing
9. watching
10. playing

Understand: Gerunds as Complements

(Page 31)

A. Complete the sentences. Use the verbs in the gerund form.
1. joining
2. skiing
3. saving
4. carrying
5. camping
6. skating
7. overeating
8. swimming
9. waiting
10. sleeping

Understand: Gerunds as Objects of Prepositions

(Page 31)

A. Choose the correct preposition.
1. in
2. of
3. of
4. to
5. on
6. on
7. for
8. on
9. with
10. about
11. by
12. at
13. with
14. for
15. in

(Page 32)

B. Choose the best verb to complete the sentences.
1. helping
2. winning
3. speeding
4. forgetting
5. cheating
6. leaving
7. investing
8. falling
9. smoking
10. copying

Understand: Gerunds vs. Infinitives

(Page 34)

A. Circle the correct form of the verb in each sentence.
1. to make
2. to have
3. to get / getting
4. to finish
5. to enter
6. spending
7. to give
8. to walk around
9. looking
10. giving
11. changing
12. to have
13. telling
14. taking / to take
15. eating / to eat

(Page 34)

B. Choose the best verb to complete the sentence.
1. mind
2. postponed
3. admitted
4. offered
5. arranged
6. risk
7. disliked
8. failed
9. claimed
10. involves

(Page 35)

C. Complete the following sentences using gerunds and infinitives.
1. not to know
2. using
3. staying
4. to be
5. doing / to do
6. to have
7. to speak up
8. going / to go
9. to tell
10. checking

Understand: "Make/Let someone do something"
(Page 36)

A. Rewrite the sentences using **make** and **let**.
1. The doctor doesn't let anyone smoke in the waiting room.
2. The story was very sad and it made me cry.
3. We do not let our children stay up after 8:00.
4. The police made the thief return the stolen money.
5. The boss made all the workers do overtime.
6. The teacher let us hand in our assignments late.
7. The parents let their teenager drive their car only on the weekends.
8. Weather conditions made us change our holiday plans.
9. The spoiled fish that we ate at dinner made everyone sick.
10. The pool supervisor doesn't let children use the pool unsupervised.

Vocabulary Challenge
(Page 36)

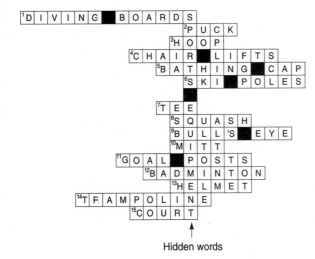

Hidden words

Unit 4

Understand: Tag Questions
(Page 43)

A. Match the statement and the tag question.
1. f
2. d
3. h
4. i
5. j
6. b
7. g
8. a
9. e
10. c

(Page 44)

B. Write tag questions for these statements.
1. wasn't it?
2. were they?
3. isn't he/she?
4. aren't you?
5. aren't they?
6. are we?
7. did he/she?
8. is it?
9. aren't I?
10. is he?

(Page 44)

C. Match the statement and the tag question.
1. d
2. h
3. e
4. g
5. j
6. b
7. f
8. c
9. a
10. i

(Page 45)

D. Write the tag questions for these statements.
1. doesn't she?
2. did he?
3. don't you?
4. don't they?
5. didn't they?
6. do they?
7. doesn't it?
8. didn't he?
9. didn't we?
10. did he?

Understand: Some Special Ways of Forming Tag Questions
(Page 46)

A. Write the tag questions for these statements.
1. isn't it?
2. was there?
3. did it?
4. didn't they?
5. did there?
6. wasn't there?
7. did they?
8. haven't they?
9. didn't they?
10. did it?

Understand: Tag Questions with Two Auxiliary Verbs
(Page 46)

A. Write the tag questions for these statements.
1. haven't they?
2. shouldn't it/they?
3. can we?
4. would they?
5. can they?
6. has it?
7. have they?
8. will it?
9. should we?
10. will we?

Understand: "I do too" and "So do I" to Agree with Affirmative Statements
(Page 47)

A. Write short statements of agreement using the auxiliary verb **do** in the correct form with **too**.
1. I did too.
2. His colleagues do too.
3. Mine does too.
4. We did too.
5. Maria did too.
6. John did too.
7. My friend did too.
8. Dan and Geoff did too.
9. Karl does too.
10. Her friend did too.

212

(Page 48)

B. Write short statements of agreement using **so** and the correct form of the auxiliary **do**.

1. So do the Nakamuras.
2. So did we.
3. So did she.
4. So does my father.
5. So do his teammates.
6. So did Sam.
7. So did Anna.
8. So do my friends and I.
9. So does ours.
10. So did I.

Understand: "I don't either" and "Neither do I" to Agree with Negative Statements

(Page 49)

A. Change the responses to the negative using **do + not + either.**

1. I won't either.
2. Mine didn't either.
3. We can't either.
4. Lynda doesn't either.
5. I didn't either.
6. Mine didn't either.
7. Tara didn't either.
8. Mine wasn't either.
9. Jun doesn't either.
10. Keiko hasn't either.

(Page 49)

B. Complete the sentences with **either** or **neither**.

1. Neither
2. either
3. Neither
4. Neither
5. either
6. either
7. either
8. Neither
9. either
10. Neither

(Page 50)

C. Find the errors and correct them.

1. Susan doesn't either.
2. Neither will I.
3. Neither did I.
4. Correct
5. Correct
6. Neither did I.
7. Correct
8. Andrea didn't either.
9. Correct
10. I don't either.

Vocabulary Challenge

(Page 50)

cards
brakes
lens
scuba-diving
rock music
mountain-biking
bowling
flash

You will remember these words in a **flash** if you study the picture dictionary, won't you?

Unit 5

TOEFL® Practice Exercises
Part A

Choose the phrase that best completes the sentence. Blacken the letter that corresponds to the answer.

1. (A) (B) (C) **(D)**
2. (A) (B) (C) **(D)**
3. (A) (B) **(C)** (D)
4. (A) (B) **(C)** (D)
5. **(A)** (B) (C) (D)
6. (A) (B) **(C)** (D)
7. (A) (B) **(C)** (D)
8. (A) **(B)** (C) (D)
9. (A) (B) **(C)** (D)
10. (A) (B) (C) **(D)**
11. (A) **(B)** (C) (D)
12. (A) **(B)** (C) (D)
13. **(A)** (B) (C) (D)
14. (A) (B) (C) **(D)**
15. (A) (B) (C) **(D)**

Score 15

Part B

Blacken the letter that corresponds to the error in the sentence.

16. **(A)** (B) (C) (D)
17. **(A)** (B) (C) (D)
18. (A) (B) (C) **(D)**
19. (A) **(B)** (C) (D)
20. **(A)** (B) (C) (D)
21. (A) **(B)** (C) (D)
22. (A) **(B)** (C) (D)
23. (A) (B) **(C)** (D)
24. **(A)** (B) (C) (D)
25. **(A)** (B) (C) (D)
26. (A) (B) **(C)** (D)
27. (A) **(B)** (C) (D)
28. (A) (B) (C) **(D)**
29. (A) (B) **(C)** (D)
30. (A) **(B)** (C) (D)
31. (A) (B) **(C)** (D)
32. (A) (B) (C) **(D)**
33. (A) (B) **(C)** (D)
34. (A) **(B)** (C) (D)
35. **(A)** (B) (C) (D)
36. (A) (B) **(C)** (D)
37. (A) (B) **(C)** (D)
38. (A) **(B)** (C) (D)
39. (A) (B) **(C)** (D)
40. (A) (B) **(C)** (D)

Score 25

Unit 6

Understand: Past Perfect Aspect
(Page 62)

A. Complete the sentences using the past perfect form of the verb.

1. had lost
2. had flown
3. had gone
4. had driven
5. had won
6. had worked
7. had lost
8. had handed in
9. had escaped
10. had eaten

(Page 63)

B. Choose the best verb to complete the sentences.

1. had already played
2. had already had
3. had already stopped
4. had already gone
5. had already put out
6. had already left
7. had already started
8. had already been married
9. had already been
10. had already turned down

Understand: Past Perfect with Expressions of Time
(Page 64)

A. Choose the best word to complete the sentence.

1. when
2. before
3. After
4. when
5. when
6. before
7. when
8. when
9. after
10. when

Understand: Past Perfect with "By the time"
(Page 65)

A. Combine the following pairs of sentences using **by the time.**

1. By the time she lost the election, she had been prime minister for ten years.
2. By the time he learned to speak English, he had been in Australia for one year.
3. By the time the painter was 80 years old, he had painted hundreds of paintings.
4. By the time the hitchhiker got to his destination, he had been on the road for three days.
5. By the time we finished the project in Thailand, we had worked on it for a year.
6. They had all finished writing the difficult math exam by the time the bell rang.
7. The paramedics had finished their work by the time the ambulance arrived.
8. They had played 36 holes of golf by the time it started to rain.
9. By the time my appetizer came to the table, everyone else had finished theirs.
10. She had waited in the rain for fifteen minutes by the time the bus finally arrived.

Understand: Past Perfect Aspect Negative Form
(Page 66)

A. Complete the sentences using the negative form of the past perfect.

1. he had not been
2. he had never tasted
3. The police officer had not finished
4. We had not lived
5. The guests had not unpacked
6. The sales representative had not worked
7. The famous couple had not told
8. We had not finished
9. Karine had never seen
10. Bob and Maggie had not known

Past Perfect Aspect Question Form
(Page 67)

A. Match the statements and the questions.

1. f
2. h
3. d
4. j
5. e
6. b
7. c
8. a
9. i
10. g

Understand: "Hope" and "Wish"

Hope
(Page 68)

A. Match the situations with the responses.

1. d
2. c
3. i
4. f
5. a
6. e
7. j
8. b
9. g
10. h

(Page 68)

B. Match the pictures with the questions.

1. i
2. f
3. d
4. g
5. h
6. e
7. a
8. c
9. b

(Page 69)

C. Give responses to the questions above with **I hope so** or **I hope not**.

1. I hope not.
2. I hope not.
3. I hope so.
4. I hope not.
5. I hope so.
6. I hope not.
7. I hope not.
8. I hope so.
9. I hope so.

Wish
(Page 70)

A. Complete the sentence with the correct form of the verb (**did** or **had**).

1. I wish we did. (have enough time to finish)
2. I wish they could. (speak English well)
3. The farmers wish it would. (rain)
4. We wish we had. (had something to eat at noon)
5. I wish I did. (go to meetings often)
6. They wish they hadn't. (fallen asleep during the speech)
7. I wish I hadn't. (stayed up very late last night)
8. I wish you did. (agree with me)
9. I wish I could. (remember how to get there)
10. I wish I had. (worn my rubber boots)

Vocabulary Challenge
(Page 71)

earthquake	leak
flood	overflow
tornado	plunger
blizzard	plumber
hurricane	pipe wrench

hose	ambulance
axe	paramedics
fire hydrant	stretcher
fire extinguisher	sling
ladder	crutches

flat tire
tow truck
winch
accident
skid-marks

Unit 7

Understand: Conditional I
(Page 77)

A. Match the clauses to make logical sentences.

1.	j	6.	c
2.	i	7.	g
3.	e	8.	d
4.	h	9.	f
5.	b	10.	a

Conditional I Negative Form
(Page 78)

A. Choose the correct clause to complete these sentences.

1.	b	6.	a
2.	a	7.	a
3.	b	8.	a
4.	b	9.	a
5.	b	10.	a

Conditional I Question Form
(Page 79)

A. Match the two parts of the sentence.

1.	d	6.	c
2.	a	7.	h
3.	f	8.	j
4.	b	9.	i
5.	e	10.	g

Understand: "Unless" in Conditional Sentences
(Page 80)

A. Rewrite these sentences using **unless**.

1. Unless I finish this project, I can't take a holiday.
2. Unless you have a good knowledge of English, you can't apply for the job.
3. Unless we have receipts, we can't return the merchandise.
4. Unless the children finish their vegetables, they won't get dessert.
5. Unless the smokers put out their cigarettes, they can't enter the conference room.
6. Unless people have jobs, the bank won't give them loans.
7. Unless I pass the TOEFL exam, I will not be able to get into university.
8. Unless people are wearing formal clothes, the restaurant won't let them in.
9. Unless we take care of the environment, the planet will not survive.
10. Unless everyone is present, the exam will not start.

(Page 80)

B. Use your own ideas to complete the sentences using **unless**.

Ask the teacher to check the grammar.

Understand: Conditional II
(Page 81)

A. Decide which situations will probably happen and which probably won't happen.

1.	✗	6.	✔
2.	✗	7.	✗
3.	✔	8.	✔
4.	✔	9.	✗
5.	✔	10.	✗

(Page 81)

B. Complete the sentences with things you would like to do.

Use your own ideas. Check the grammar with the teacher.

Conditional II Negative Form
(Page 82)

A. Make one clause negative so the sentences will be logical.
1. If the weather were better, we wouldn't stay at home.
2. If English weren't difficult, we would learn it quickly.
3. If she weren't worried about her grades, she would be relaxed.
4. If the air were cleaner, we wouldn't have trouble with our health.
5. If all countries were peaceful, we wouldn't have conflict.
6. If I weren't busy, I would have time to socialize.
7. If you weren't sick, you would feel good.
8. If my life weren't hectic, I would have lots of free time.
9. If we were not in financial difficulties, we wouldn't have to spend less.
10. If they weren't impolite and selfish, they would have a lot of friends.

Conditional II Question Form
(Page 83)

A. Use your own ideas to complete the questions.

Possible answers:
1. …would you do?
2. …would you go?
3. …would you spend it?
4. …you lost your keys?
5. …you couldn't speak?
6. …would you spend your time?
7. …would you be?
8. …you could have anything you wanted?
9. …you were lost in the woods?
10. …would you go?

Understand: Conditional III
(Page 83)

A. Match the sentences with the ones that follow.
1. e
2. g
3. h
4. j
5. d
6. a
7. c
8. b
9. f
10. i

(Page 84)

B. Complete the sentences with your own ideas.

Use your own ideas. Check the grammar with the teacher.

Vocabulary Challenge
(Page 85)
1. c
2. c
3. b
4. a
5. b
6. a
7. c
8. a
9. b
10. b

Unit 8
What Do You Know?
(Page 89)
1. e
2. a
3. f
4. b
5. d
6. c
7. h
8. g

Understand: Expressing Possibility and Probability with Modals
(Page 92)

A. Complete the following sentences with verbs from the list.
1. know
2. be
3. remember
4. become
5. understand
6. arrive
7. have
8. open
9. do
10. take

(Page 93)

B. Change the verb phrases in these sentences to refer to past time.
1. could have been
2. must have been
3. might have won
4. should have left
5. may have been
6. could have telephoned
7. might have broken down
8. could have misunderstood
9. should have worn
10. must have been
11. could have been elected
12. might have forgotten
13. must have been
14. should have won
15. may have been

(Page 93)

C. Match the the sentences.
1. g
2. d
3. j
4. h
5. a
6. i
7. c
8. f
9. e
10. b

216

Understand: Negative Possibility with Modals
(Page 94)

A. Use the modal and the main verb and write the negative verb phrase in the past form.
1. must not have been
2. could not have gone
3. may not have tried
4. might not have arrived
5. should not have thought
6. could not have left
7. may not have eaten
8. must not have written
9. could not have sent
10. might not have won
11. should not have said
12. may not have taken
13. must not have had
14. might not have known
15. should not have understood
16. could not have ridden
17. may not have driven
18. must not have grown
19. might not have given
20. should not have forgotten

(Page 95)

B. Read the situations below. Choose the conclusion that is the most probable.
1. b
2. a
3. a
4. a
5. a
6. a
7. a
8. b
9. a
10. a

Understand: "Must" for Deductions
(Page 96)

A. Write deductions based on the information given in brackets.
1. He must have a headache.
2. She must be sleepy.
3. He must be full.
4. He must be a weightlifter.
5. It must want to go outside.
6. They must be lost.
7. It must be dust.
8. She must have a bad cold.
9. It must be an apple pie.
10. It must be warm outside.
11. She must be absent.
12. It must be hungry.
13. She must be cold.
14. He must be tired.
15. She must want to be taller.

(Page 97)

B. Write deductions using the information in brackets.
1. It must have been raining.
2. He must have been late.
3. They must have had their dinner.
4. He must have lost (forgotten) his keys.
5. He must have had an accident.
6. He must have hurt his foot.
7. They must have heard some bad news.
8. She must have been at home.
9. She must have been stiff.
10. They must have had some good news.
11. She must have seen a ghost.
12. She must have slept in.
13. He must have heard a noise.
14. It must have snowed.
15. He/she must have been busy.

(Page 98)

C. Look at the pictures and write deductions.
Possible answers:
1. She must have been exercising.
2. They must have been swimming.
3. The dog must have been chasing the cat.
4. They must have been eating pizza.
5. They must have been waiting a long time.
6. They must have been talking a long time.
7. They must have been dancing for a long time.
8. Someone must have been driving too fast.
9. He must have been studying late.

Understand: "Had better"
(Page 100)

A. Match the situations and advice using had better.
1. d
2. e
3. i
4. h
5. f
6. a
7. c
8. b
9. g
10. j

(Page 101)

B. Choose the best verb to complete the sentence. Use the negative form.
1. not spend
2. not stay
3. not speak
4. not arrive
5. not make
6. not eat
7. not go
8. not drive
9. not take
10. not forget
11. not try
12. not play
13. not get
14. not wear
15. not ask for

Vocabulary Challenge

(Page 102)

pumps	sole
sling backs	heel
high heels	toe
zipper	nail file
velcro	emery board
buttons	nail clipper
turtle neck	collar
V-neck	sleeve
crew neck	cuff
striped	chain
checked	bracelet
polka dots	necklace
pyjamas	
nightgown	
bathrobe	

Ten-Minute Grammar Games

Solve the Problems

(Page 102)

1. When they pass each other, they are equal distance from the stadium.
2. He needs to pull out at least three socks to ensure that he will make a matching pair. If the second sock doesn't match the first sock, the third sock will match either the first or the second. To ensure that he will be able to make a blue set, he needs to pull out 13 socks, because the first 12 could possibly all be black.

Unit 9

Understand: Direct Speech

(Page 106)

A. Punctuate the following sentences correctly.

1. Neil Armstrong said, "One small step for man, one giant step for mankind."
2. Albert Einstein said, "Energy equals mass, times the speed of light, squared."
3. Ann Landers said, "People who drink to drown their sorrows should be told that sorrows know how to swim."
4. A well-known proverb says, "Never put off until tomorrow what you can do today."
5. A famous bumper sticker says, "Don't follow me, I'm lost."
6. Benjamin Disraeli said, "The reason you have one mouth and two ears is so you can listen twice as much as you talk."
7. Confucius said, "To know the road ahead, ask someone who is coming back."
8. Victor Hugo said, "No army can stop an idea whose time has come."

9. An Arabian proverb says, "If the camel gets its nose in the tent, its body will soon follow."
10. Al Capone once said, "I don't even know what street Canada is on."

(Page 107)

B. Match the introductory statements with the words that probably followed them.

1.	d	6.	i
2.	c	7.	e
3.	a	8.	f
4.	g	9.	b
5.	h	10.	j

(Page 107)

C. Write the sentences out as direct speech with appropriate punctuation.

1. The teacher said, "You may turn over your papers and begin the exam now."
2. The doctor advised, "Smoking has been shown to contribute to cancer."
3. The coach threatened, "Anyone who is caught smoking will be off the team."
4. The flight attendant said, "Please make sure your seat belts are fastened securely."
5. The head nurse asked, "Is there anyone here who can work a double shift today?"
6. The tourist inquired, "Is this the right bus for the Eiffel Tower?"
7. The angry police officer shouted, "Show me your driver's licence and registration."
8. The taxi driver asked, "Where would you like to go?"
9. The travel agent explained, "Lower seat rates are in effect as of next week."
10. The personnel officer asked, "Do you have any experience in international law?"

Understand: Indirect Speech

Verb Changes

(Page 108)

A. Change the sentences to indirect speech with **that** and the appropriate change of tense.

1. The artist said that watercolours were easy to use.
2. The teacher said that the exam tomorrow would be difficult.
3. John said that people didn't like the idea of getting home late.
4. Angela said that tourists couldn't find the bus station easily.
5. The ringmaster said that the acrobats would ride on the elephants.
6. The driver said that the bus wouldn't go until everyone was on board.
7. Mrs. Tang said that the weather had been terrible in England.

8. The tourist said that Paris was a beautiful city to visit.
9. Mr. Dupont said that the musicians weren't going to be happy in an old concert hall.
10. The conductor said that everyone needed to tune their instruments.
11. An actress said that the theatre was the highest form of art.
12. The singer said that not everyone would agree with that statement.
13. My teacher said that students everywhere were the same.
14. Francisco said that everyone had really enjoyed the performance.
15. Mary said that cats didn't generally like water very much.

Adverbial Changes
(Page 109)

A. Change the sentences to indirect speech. Make changes to the verbs. Make changes to the adverbials or demonstratives.

1. I said that I thought the piano was out of tune **that night**.
2. We said that we had really enjoyed the party **the day before**.
3. I said that I didn't want to park my car near **that one**.
4. My boss and I said that we planned to open a factory **there the following year**.
5. We said that we could change places **the following morning**.
6. My fiance and I said that we were going to be married **the following year**.
7. I said that I was going to buy that car **the following day**.
8. I said that I was taking tuba lessons **there then**.
9. Jim and I said that we had studied saxophone **there** for six months.
10. I said that I would meet you **the following week**.

Pronoun Changes
(Page 110)

A. Put the correct pronouns in the following sentences.

1. I
2. he
3. I/we I/we
4. she our
5. their
6. I my
7. we
8. she
9. he/she us
10. I his

(Page 110)

B. Change the sentences to indirect speech. Make all the necessary changes.

1. They replied that it was too cold there.
2. Maria replied that she had seen enough of that movie.
3. My boss announced that anyone who was late would be fired.
4. The hungry teenager complained that she/he wanted to eat something then.
5. Their mother said that it was too late to watch TV then.
6. The conductor said we could all fit onto the stage easily.
7. The tour guide said that we would be late if we didn't leave for the play then.
8. Our boss announced that employees were not allowed to park there without permits.
9. Someone suggested that we should leave there that night.
10. Mike said that he thought that everyone should leave there the next day.

Understand: Questions in Indirect Speech
(Page 111)
Yes/No Questions

A. Report on the following yes/no questions using indirect speech.

1. My aunt asked if (whether) we were on time for the concert.
2. The tourist asked if (whether) that was the train for New York.
3. Suzanne asked if (whether) those jackets were on sale that day.
4. My grandmother asked if (whether) the violin was out of tune.
5. The teacher asked if (whether) that was the best work the class could do.
6. My friend asked if (whether) there was another movie we could watch.
7. The man I met in the hall asked if (whether) we were next-door neighbours.
8. The math teacher asked if (whether) my brother and I were twins.
9. The lion tamer asked if (whether) there were any more lions in the cage.
10. My mother-in-law asked if (whether) that was an oil painting.

WH-Questions
(Page 112)

A. Report on these questions in indirect speech.

1. The tourist wondered when the next bus left.
2. My friend asked how long the trip to Boston was.
3. The grouch asked why there was such a long delay.

4. The magician asked where he had put his rabbit.
5. The desk clerk asked what time they would arrive.
6. The club president asked when we could get together.
7. The visitor asked what that sign meant.
8. The doctor asked how I had been feeling.
9. Susan asked what that delicious cake was made of.
10. The new employee asked how often he needed to wear a tie.

Understand: Imperatives in Indirect Speech
Affirmative Imperative
(Page 112)

A. Change the reports of imperative statements into indirect speech.
1. The mother ordered the naughty children to go to bed.
2. The police officer ordered the burglar to go out of the basement.
3. One student asked another student to pass the pencil sharpener.
4. Our teacher advised us to check the answers carefully.
5. The bank teller told me to sign the back of the cheque.
6. The radio announcer advised the public to be careful of the water.
7. The father told his son to be home by eleven o'clock, or else.
8. The bank robber told the teller to hand over the cash quickly.
9. The teacher told the students to wait in the corridor.
10. The art student told her sister to leave her paintbrushes alone.

Negative Imperative
(Page 113)

A. Write sentences using the negative imperative for reporting with indirect speech.
1. The ringmaster told the audience not to be afraid.
2. The usher warned the people buying tickets not to be late for the concert.
3. Sylvie told her friends not to worry about anything.
4. The doctor advised the woman not to smoke.
5. The conductor warned the violinist not to play too fast.
6. Mario told his brother not to use the bike without asking.
7. The police officer told the driver not to turn left at the corner.
8. Keiko told her family not to send any letters after June 1.

9. Pierre told his wife not to forget to buy gas on the way home.
10. Everyone advised us not to go to Hawaii in the summer.

Understand: "Say" and "Tell"
(Page 113)

A. Change the verb **say** to **tell** and identify the person who was spoken to.
1. The speaker told the audience that a cure for the disease could be found in about ten years.
2. The computer salesman told the customer that the model she wanted to buy was obsolete.
3. The psychologist told the patient that this form of behaviour was generally easy to modify.
4. The hostess told the guests that coffee would be served in the living room after dinner.
5. The police chief told the journalists that crime had decreased in certain neighbourhoods.
6. The professor told the students that the research project would have to be at least 20 pages long.
7. The sales manager told the sales representatives that the new styles would be in by the following week.
8. The film director told the actress that the movie would be sure to make millions of dollars.
9. The adoption agency told the couple that the baby would be available in two months time.
10. The teacher told the students that there would be a very difficult exam and that they should study hard.

(Page 114)

B. Complete the sentences with the name of the person who was spoken to.
1. his mother
2. the cat
3. the passengers
4. the customers
5. the teacher
6. the soldier
7. her room-mate
8. the visitors
9. the juggler
10. the children

Vocabulary Challenge
Who Said It?
(Page 115)
1. violinist, guitarist, cellist
2. conductor
3. magician
4. clown
5. contortionist
6. musician
7. pianist
8. trapeze artist
9. juggler
10. lion tamer

What Am I?
(Page 115)

1. cello
2. piano
3. canvas
4. sheet music
5. harmonica
6. baton
7. charcoal
8. flute
9. drum
10. frame

Ten-Minute Grammar Games
Medieval Puzzles
(Page 116)

1. b
2. d
3. a
4. f
5. c
6. e

Unit 10

TOEFL® Practice Exercises

Part A

Choose the phrase that best completes the sentence. Blacken the letter that corresponds to the answer.

1. (A) (B) (C) **(D)**
2. **(A)** (B) (C) (D)
3. (A) **(B)** (C) (D)
4. (A) (B) **(C)** (D)
5. **(A)** (B) (C) (D)
6. (A) **(B)** (C) (D)
7. (A) (B) (C) **(D)**
8. (A) (B) **(C)** (D)
9. (A) (B) (C) **(D)**
10. (A) (B) (C) **(D)**
11. (A) (B) **(C)** (D)
12. (A) (B) **(C)** (D)
13. (A) (B) (C) **(D)**
14. (A) **(B)** (C) (D)
15. **(A)** (B) (C) (D)

Score 15

Part B

Blacken the letter that corresponds to the error in the sentence.

16. (A) **(B)** (C) (D)
17. **(A)** (B) (C) (D)
18. (A) **(B)** (C) (D)
19. (A) (B) **(C)** (D)
20. (A) (B) (C) **(D)**
21. (A) (B) (C) **(D)**
22. (A) (B) **(C)** (D)
23. **(A)** (B) (C) (D)
24. **(A)** (B) (C) (D)
25. (A) (B) **(C)** (D)

26. **(A)** (B) (C) (D)
27. (A) (B) **(C)** (D)
28. (A) (B) (C) **(D)**
29. **(A)** (B) (C) (D)
30. **(A)** (B) (C) (D)
31. (A) **(B)** (C) (D)
32. (A) **(B)** (C) (D)
33. (A) (B) **(C)** (D)
34. **(A)** (B) (C) (D)
35. **(A)** (B) (C) (D)
36. **(A)** (B) (C) (D)
37. **(A)** (B) (C) (D)
38. (A) **(B)** (C) (D)
39. **(A)** (B) (C) (D)
40. (A) (B) (C) **(D)**

Score 25

Unit 11

What Do You Know?
(Page 127)

1. b
2. a
3. a
4. c
5. a
6. b
7. a
8. a
9. c
10. b

Understand: Passive Voice
(Page 130)

A. Give the passive form of the verbs in the tense indicated.

1. we were inspected
2. they will be identified
3. I am recorded
4. she is served
5. you were telephoned
6. he will be observed
7. they were admired
8. we will be received
9. I was excluded
10. it will be opened
11. he was told
12. she was refused
13. he is protected
14. it will be developed
15. I will be followed
16. you are met
17. you were hurt
18. he will be married
19. we were sent
20. he was reprimanded

(Page 130)

B. Change these sentences to the passive voice. Omit the doer.

1. The story was reported last weekend.
2. The best-selling novel was translated last year.
3. The patient will be examined in approximately one hour.
4. The new system was installed last year.
5. Hundreds of new recordings are put out every month.
6. Solemn promises are broken all the time.
7. The leaky faucet was repaired in just a few minutes.
8. The outside of their house was painted only last year.
9. The stitches will be removed this afternoon.
10. Spanish is spoken in many countries in the world.
11. The money will be transferred electronically in a few hours.
12. Rice is grown in many countries around the world.
13. The sunken pirate ship was located in 1986.
14. A delicious dinner was served in the dining room.
15. Over one hundred goals were scored last season.

(Page 131)

C. Change these sentences to the active voice.

1. That teacher corrected the papers very quickly.
2. The customs officer inspected my bag at the counter.
3. The writer will write the book by next summer.
4. The sales manager presents a report to the president every month.
5. Garbage trucks pick up garbage every two days.
6. Doctors treated many people for burns after the fire.
7. The judge sentenced the criminal to life in prison.
8. The hospital will lay off many nurses next year.
9. Farmers sighted an unidentified flying object recently.
10. Engineers carry out checks of nuclear waste sites often.
11. The magician impressed the children with magic tricks.
12. The storm knocked down the telephone lines.
13. Jane took some beautiful pictures of Niagara Falls.
14. Two armed men robbed the bank yesterday morning.
15. An orderly brought the patient to the ward in a wheelchair.

Understand: When to Use the Passive Voice
(Page 132)

A. Identify the recipient of the action in the following sentences.

1. the application form
2. the injured man
3. many buildings
4. tea and coffee
5. the forest fire
6. smoke detectors
7. the patient's pulse
8. the suspect
9. the speech
10. the accident
11. the witness
12. unusual stories
13. a public announcement
14. first aid
15. the scene of the disaster

(Page 132)

B. Choose the sentence that is correct. Indicate whether it is active or passive.

1. b P	9. b P
2. a A	10. a A
3. b P	11. a A
4. b P	12. b P
5. b P	13. b P
6. a A	14. b P
7. b P	15. b P
8. a A	

Understand: The Passive Voice with "By"
(Page 134)

Cross out doers that are unnecessary in the sentences.

1. by a manufacturer	9. ✔
2. by EFL teachers	10. ✔
3. ✔	11. by chickens
4. by farmers	12. ✔
5. by researchers	13. by the teacher
6. ✔	14. ✔
7. by players	15. by a waiter
8. by a poet	

Understand: Present and Past Participles Used as Adjectives
(Page 135)

A. Choose the correct form of the participle.

1. interesting	6. disappointing
2. dominating	7. depressing
3. frightened	8. embarrassing
4. satisfying	9. surprised
5. confusing	10. irritating

222

(Page 135)

B. Complete the sentences with the correct participle.

1. puzzling
2. irritated
3. excited
4. shocking
5. amusing
6. boring
7. disgusted
8. insulted
9. amazing
10. worried

Vocabulary Challenge
(Page 136)

Hidden message

Unit 12

What Do You Know?
(Page 141)

1. olive
2. strawberry
3. chocolate
4. almond
5. grapefruit

Understand: Passive Voice with the Continuous Aspect
(Page 142)

A. Write the verbs below in the passive form.

1. are being exposed
2. was being watched
3. is being controlled
4. are being manufactured
5. is being produced
6. was being planned
7. were being discovered
8. am being sent
9. is being forgotten
10. were being remembered

11. is being damaged
12. are being painted
13. were being studied
14. is being written
15. was being examined
16. was being employed
17. are being discriminated
18. was being reviewed
19. were being improved
20. am being helped

(Page 143)

B. Write the following sentences in the passive voice.

1. The candidate is being interviewed now.
2. The burglary suspect is being interrogated.
3. Our favourite restaurant is being remodelled.
4. Their old car is being repaired.
5. The contract is being signed.
6. My new party dress is being shortened.
7. The front door is being painted.
8. My neighbour is already being helped.
9. The bank is being held up.
10. The house is still being built.

(Page 143)

C. Write the sentences in the active voice. Use the words in brackets as the subject of the sentence.

1. The social committee was organizing the New Year's party.
2. The kitchen staff were chopping the walnuts and pecans.
3. The lifeguard was giving mouth-to-mouth resuscitation to the swimmer.
4. The team doctor was testing the athletes for drug use.
5. A nurse was caring for the elderly woman.
6. Burn specialists were treating the firefighter for burns.
7. The restaurant was asking the cooks to do too much overtime.
8. Housekeepers were cleaning the hotel rooms.
9. The secretary was sending the fax in the other office.
10. The teacher was keeping the math class in after school.

Understand: Passive Voice with the Perfective Aspect
(Page 144)

A. Change the simple passive to the perfective passive.

1. It has been done before.
2. They have been selected for the job.
3. It has been translated into many languages.

4. It has been hidden from sight.
5. We have been criticized for it.
6. They have been shown many samples.
7. She has been told that she was right.
8. It has been noticed by several people.
9. It has been broken.
10. It has been tried before.

(Page 144)

B. Write these sentences in the past perfect passive form. Omit mention of the doer.
1. Many foreign leaders had been consulted.
2. The report had been written before the due date.
3. The sink had not been fixed before we moved in.
4. Many meals for homeless people had been provided.
5. A petition against the project had been circulated.
6. Our flight had been announced twice before we heard it.
7. Everyone had been shocked by news of the terrible accident.
8. Many different experiments had been conducted.
9. At least 50 new employees had been hired.
10. The exam schedules for the fall term had been announced.

(Page 145)

C. Complete the sentences with the verbs below.
1. had been washed
2. has been resolved
3. had been edited
4. has been postponed
5. had been sent
6. have been fascinated
7. had been filled in
8. had been held
9. had been filled
10. had been read over

Understand: Passive Voice and Future Time with "Be going to"
(Page 145)

A. Put the verb phrases in the passive voice with **be going to** (for future time).
1. is going to be turned off
2. is going to be opened
3. is going to be mailed
4. are going to be posted
5. are going to be married
6. are going to be ground
7. are going to be sampled
8. are going to be packed
9. are going to be invited
10. is going to be included

(Page 146)

B. Look at the pictures and write a passive sentence with **be going to**.

1. The fish is going to be caught.
2. The pickpocket is going to be arrested.
3. The letter carrier is going to be bitten by the dog.
4. The car is going to be towed away.
5. The TV is going to be turned off.
6. The garbage is going to be collected.
7. The windows are going to be washed.
8. The food is going to be served.
9. The birthday candles are going to be blown out.

"Would rather" When the Subject Does Not Change
(Page 147)

A. Make sentences comparing two activities with **I'd rather... than**. Use the activity in bold type as your preference.
1. I'd rather go to the film festival than go to a baseball game.
2. I'd rather stay home than go out this evening.
3. I'd rather have a soft drink than have a fruit juice.
4. I'd rather take a plane than take a train.
5. I'd rather read a book than play computer games.
6. I'd rather go to the beach than go on a tour.
7. I'd rather sleep late on weekends than get up early on weekends.
8. I'd rather be poor and happy than be rich and unhappy.
9. I'd rather order take-out food than cook dinner myself.
10. I'd rather eat artichokes than eat broccoli.

(Page 147)

B. Complete the sentences with your own ideas.

Check the grammar with your teacher.

"Would rather" When the Subject Changes
(Page 148)

A. Choose the best verb to complete the sentence. Put it in the correct tense.
1. wrote
2. cooked
3. consulted
4. did not put
5. came
6. took
7. did not give
8. did not find out
9. cancelled
10. sent

(Page 149)

B. Fill in the blanks with the verbs in present or past time.
1. No, I'd rather you called them.
2. No, I'd rather do it myself.
3. I would rather you didn't smoke anywhere in the house.
4. I'd rather go by myself.
5. Yes. I'd rather you didn't try to fix it yourself.

6. I would rather you waited a few more days.
7. I'd rather everyone came alone.
8. I'm really tired. I'd rather go straight home.
9. I'd rather they didn't start until everyone is ready.
10. I'd rather you didn't spend any more money for a while.

Vocabulary Challenge
(Page 150)

Unit 13

Understand: Causative Statements with "Have"
Both Causer and Doer Are Mentioned
(Page 156)

A. Identify the causer and the doer in the sentences below.
1. the driver, the mechanic
2. the lawyer, her assistant
3. the children's parents, the dentist
4. the cadet, the military barber
5. the exhausted tourist, the waiter
6. the homeroom teacher, the students
7. Mrs. Williams, her son
8. the priest, the bride and groom
9. Fred Burns, the coffee shop
10. Mr. Tanaka, room service

(Page 157)

B. Complete the sentences by choosing a doer from the list below.
1. the company   6. the landlord
2. the players   7. the students
3. a cleaning service   8. the criminal
4. patients   9. the actors
5. my brothers   10. a hairdresser

Only the Causer Is Mentioned
(Page 157)

A. Rewrite the sentences omitting mention of the doer and making necessary changes.
1. The Johnsons are having their house redecorated.
2. Mario has his blood pressure checked every week.
3. Professor Jones will have his manuscript proofread before he sends it to the publisher.
4. The famous actress had her portrait painted.
5. The manufacturer has the cars checked before they leave the factory.
6. Michael Grey had his new pants shortened.
7. My neighbours are having their old windows replaced.
8. Francine is having her car repaired this week.
9. Susy had her cat looked after while she was away.
10. Jackson had his dinner brought to his room.

Understand: Causative Statements with "Get"
(Page 158)

A. Make causative statements using these elements and **get** (**got**).
1. Janet got her sister to lend her a sweater.
2. The coach got the players to train harder.
3. The wife got the husband to do the shopping. (The husband got the wife to do the shopping).
4. The teacher got a student to erase the board.
5. The telephone company got the deadbeat to pay the bill.
6. Paula got her boyfriend Fred to marry her.
7. Gaby got her roommate to wash the dishes.
8. My friend got me to type her essay.
9. The clown got the children to smile.
10. The music teacher got her students to practise the piano.

(Page 159)

B. Choose the person who was probably the doer in these sentences.
1. a mechanic   6. an orthodontist
2. the judge   7. the vet
3. the gardener   8. a plumber
4. an architect   9. a carpenter
5. a lawyer   10. a locksmith

(Page 160)

C. Go back to the previous exercise and use the information to write causative statements with **got**.
1. They got a mechanic to change their tires.
2. The lawyer got the judge to reduce the fine.
3. She got the gardener to plant the flowers.
4. They got an architect to design the house.
5. She got a lawyer to make her will.
6. He got an orthodontist to examine his teeth.

7. She got the vet to vaccinate her pet.
8. We got a plumber to fix our kitchen sink.
9. You got a carpenter to repair the furniture.
10. They got a locksmith to make a car key.

Understand: Use of the Verb "Make"
(Page 160)

A. Match each of the actions to a category.

1. e	8. e	15. b
2. d	9. a	16. e
3. c	10. d	17. a
4. c	11. c	18. d
5. e	12. e	19. b
6. d	13. e	20. e
7. d/a	14. a	

Understand: "Make" and "Do"
(Page 162)

A. Complete the sentences with **make** or **do**. Put the verb in the correct tense.

1. has been doing	9. made
2. making	10. do
3. has been doing	11. do
4. made	12. made
5. makes	13. have done
6. are doing	14. have made
7. are making	15. done
8. did	

Vocabulary Challenge
(Page 162)

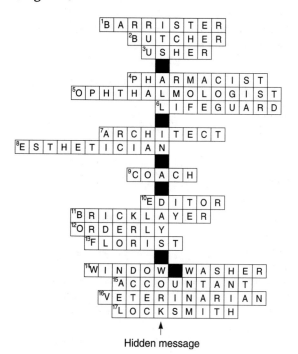

Hidden message

Unit 14

Understand: Yes/No Questions
Inversion of Word Order
(Page 168)

A. Change these sentences to question form.
1. Can Anna relax on the weekend?
2. Has François walked around the block twice?
3. Would Lin buy a new car if he had the money?
4. Should Poling take a couple of computer courses?
5. Were you embarrassed by all the attention?
6. Will the show begin at eight o'clock sharp?
7. Was a poster put up at the end of the hall?
8. Had the game started before we arrived?
9. Are they studying for the TOEFL exam?
10. Could George Washington speak French?
11. Was that movie seen by many people?
12. Has Joe been working there for a long time?
13. Have my friends gone to Toronto?
14. Have Sue and Jun bought a new car?
15. Was Max working in a skyscraper last year?

Use of the Dummy Auxiliary "Do"
(Page 169)

A. Change these sentences to question form.
1. Do your neighbours like to sit on the balcony every evening?
2. Do your best friends live next door to you?
3. Does Sarah speak five European languages?
4. Did Jack call Mimi from a phone booth?
5. Do the Dunns ride horses on the weekend?
6. Was there a lot of litter in the park?
7. Does this billboard attract a lot of attention?
8. Did Maxine leave the front door unlocked?
9. Do revolving doors help conserve energy in buildings?
10. Does the subway stop running at 11:00?
11. Did the children cross the street at the crosswalk?
12. Did you see a lot of neon signs in the city?
13. Did Milo say that he liked opera?
14. Does Mike swim before breakfast every day?
15. Do ambulances and police cars both have sirens?

Understand: Short Answers
(Page 170)

A. Complete the answers to the questions with short answer form.

1. No, she hasn't.	6. No, they haven't.
2. Yes, they were,	7. Yes, I did.
3. No, they won't.	8. No, she wasn't.
4. No, I can't,	9. Yes, he is.
5. Yes, I do.	10. No, I haven't.

Understand: Negative Questions
(Page 171)

A. Match the questions and the answers.

1.	d	9.	n
2.	g	10.	m
3.	e	11.	o
4.	f	12.	l
5.	j	13.	c
6.	i	14.	a
7.	h	15.	b
8.	k		

(Page 172)

B. Write negative questions. Use the appropriate auxiliary. Use contractions.

1. Doesn't Mike work in the accounting department?
2. Don't Keiko and Mei live in a high-rise apartment?
3. Doesn't Annie ever walk to work in the morning?
4. Couldn't Tim and Joan make it to the party?
5. Isn't Min Hee interested in learning judo?
6. Doesn't Alberto like swimming in the ocean?
7. Wasn't the game cancelled because of rain?
8. Hadn't Maria had supper when she got here?
9. Isn't the weather forecast ever good on weekends?
10. Hasn't Kwong had any time off this week?
11. Hasn't the janitor cleaned the graffiti off the wall?
12. Doesn't the restaurant have a neon sign?
13. Didn't we meet a lot of people at the party?
14. Shouldn't we leave for home before it's too late?
15. Hasn't Dan changed since we last saw him?

Understand: WH-Information Questions
(Page 174)

A. Complete the questions with the correct auxiliary verb.

1.	have	6.	were
2.	is	7.	have
3.	were	8.	does
4.	are	9.	have
5.	have	10.	did

(Page 174)

B. Write 15 WH-information questions based on the information in the text.

Check the grammar with your teacher.

Sample questions:
1. How often do we use herbs that have medicinal properties?
2. How do you start your day?

3. What is America's favourite morning stimulant?
4. What have scientists shown about coffee?
5. How does tea compare to coffee?
6. Why would tea help in preventing tooth decay?
7. What was the origin of most of today's carbonated beverages?
8. How long ago did the Chinese drink ginger for indigestion?

Understand: "Who" and "What" as Subjects in Questions
(Page 176)

A. Write questions using the question words **who** and **what** as subjects in the sentences.

1. What happened?
2. Who arrived quickly?
3. Who took careful notes?
4. What was called?
5. What happened to the driver?
6. Who was taken to the hospital?
7. Who arrived on the scene?
8. What was taken of the scene?
9. What was published in the paper?
10. Who read about it the next day?

(Page 176)

B. Complete the questions using **what** or **who** as the subject or object according to the context.

1. What got stolen? **S**
2. Who found her wallet? **S**
3. What did the police find? **O**
4. What will the courier bring tomorrow? **O**
5. Who will bring the package tomorrow? **S**
6. What got towed away an hour ago? **S**
7. Who is getting engaged this month? **S**
8. What did she cook for the family? **O**
9. What did they plan to visit? **O**
10. Who participated in the meeting? **S**
11. Who lived in this house? **S**
12. What drew a lot of applause? **S** or What did his speech draw? **O**
13. Who caused the accident? **S**
14. What was the speaker given? **O**
15. Who was given a round of applause? **O**

Understand: Questions with "Like"
(Page 177)

A. Match the questions with appropriate answers.

1.	g	6.	h
2.	e	7.	a
3.	j	8.	c
4.	d	9.	f
5.	b	10.	i

(Page 178)

  B. Make questions that match the answers below with **what + like**.

1. What does Leo look like?
2. What is Mieke like?
3. What does Steve like?
4. What does Charles like?
5. What is the city like?
6. What are you like?
7. What does Carolyn like?
8. What are musicians like?
9. What is Annabel like?
10. What does the Empire State Building look like?

Vocabulary Challenge
(Page 178)

1. an awning	11. pigeons
2. a walkway	12. a high-rise
3. graffiti	13. a neon sign
4. stairs	14. a mural
5. billboards, posters	15. a siren
6. a flagpole	16. a parking lot, at a meter
7. a railing	17. a traffic jam
8. a phone booth	18. a bus shelter
9. a revolving door	19. a crosswalk
10. a ramp	20. a crane

Ten-Minute Grammar Games
Solve the Problems
(Page 179)

1. Marta was born in South America, between December and March. At that time it is summer in South America. Now Marta lives in North America, so her birthday falls in winter.
2. A kilogram is a measure of weight, so a kilogram of apples weighs the same as a kilogram of feathers.
3. The survivors are alive. They would not be buried.
4. One of the coins was not a quarter, but the other coin **was** a quarter. Therefore, the person had a nickel and a quarter.
5. One stamp costs 46 cents.
6. The person is a bank teller. He never said the money was his!

TOEFL® Practice Exercises
Part A

Choose the phrase that best completes the sentence. Blacken the letter that corresponds to the answer.

1. **(A)** (B) (C) (D)
2. (A) **(B)** (C) (D)
3. (A) (B) **(C)** (D)
4. (A) (B) (C) **(D)**
5. (A) **(B)** (C) (D)
6. (A) (B) (C) **(D)**
7. (A) (B) (C) **(D)**
8. (A) (B) **(C)** (D)
9. (A) **(B)** (C) (D)
10. **(A)** (B) (C) (D)
11. (A) (B) (C) **(D)**
12. (A) (B) **(C)** (D)
13. (A) **(B)** (C) (D)
14. (A) (B) (C) **(D)**
15. (A) (B) **(C)** (D)

Score 15

Part B

Blacken the letter that corresponds to the error in the sentence.

16. (A) **(B)** (C) (D)
17. (A) **(B)** (C) (D)
18. (A) (B) **(C)** (D)
19. (A) **(B)** (C) (D)
20. **(A)** (B) (C) (D)
21. (A) (B) **(C)** (D)
22. (A) (B) **(C)** (D)
23. (A) (B) (C) **(D)**
24. (A) (B) **(C)** (D)
25. (A) **(B)** (C) (D)
26. **(A)** (B) (C) (D)
27. (A) (B) (C) **(D)**
28. **(A)** (B) (C) (D)
29. (A) (B) (C) **(D)**
30. (A) **(B)** (C) (D)
31. (A) (B) (C) **(D)**
32. **(A)** (B) (C) (D)
33. (A) **(B)** (C) (D)
34. (A) (B) (C) **(D)**
35. (A) (B) (C) **(D)**
36. (A) (B) (C) **(D)**
37. (A) (B) **(C)** (D)
38. (A) (B) **(C)** (D)
39. (A) (B) (C) **(D)**
40. (A) **(B)** (C) (D)

Score 25

DATE DE RETOUR